INCREASING SALES EFFECTIVENESS

A COMPLETE GUIDE TO A SUCCESSFUL SELLING PROGRAM

by

JOSEPH S. SANCHEZ, M.B.A.

PUBLISHED BY

FERIS-LEE, PRESS

LODI, NEW JERSEY

To my beloved mother, Perla, who provided me
with courage and wisdom.

Library of Congress Cataloging in Publication Data

Sanchez, Joseph S.
  Increasing sales effectiveness.

  Bibliography: p.
  1. Selling. 2. Sales management. I. Title.
HF5438.25.S26 1987   658.8'1   87-8794
ISBN 0-941315-14-2

Edited by: Lynda M. Tua

Typeset by: Sara Nicoll

TABLE OF CONTENTS

PART ONE
THE ECONOMICS OF SELLING

PART TWO
THE SALES STAFF

PART THREE

THE SELLING PROGRAM

PART FOUR

SPECIALIZED SALES PROGRAMS

INTRODUCTION

Today's changing business environment demands that executives re-evaluate their business philosophy and sales approach rather than conducting business as usual. What has been successful in the past may not produce the same results today for a myriad of reasons. The marketplace is constantly subject to change because of new competitors, new product applications, new improved products, and the increasing cost of manufacturing products. Even if no dramatic events were to occur, during a given year, the cost of doing business continues to increase year after year. Employees expect annual raises, taxes increase, insurance premiums increase, equipment and furniture wear out and need repair or replacement. As you can readily see, nothing stays constant. If a business is to survive it has to stay competitive, and the most important factor that allows a business to remain competitive is efficiency.

During prosperous times a firm can survive even if its expenses are much greater than the industry norm. When the money is rolling in, everyone tends to bask in the glory and lose sight of, or ignore, the inefficiencies of the corporation. Often new personnel are hired to keep up with all the new business rolling in, without much regard to the consequences when business activities slow down.

The selling activity of any firm plays an intricate role in the success or failure of its product or service. Merely adding new sales personnel (I will throughout this book refer to male gender for simplicity purposes only) in the hopes of saturating the marketplace, and betting on the sheer percentages of the probability of picking up new customers is clearly not the best use of time and money. No selling plan is etched in stone. Plans should be made and reviewed at least every six months. Adjustments should be made if deemed necessary. Because conditions change, strategies sometimes do not work as well as originally hoped and personnel sometimes do not perform as anticipated because of various factors. It is because nothing stays constant that management must always be on the lookout for new methods or angles, finding new areas where operations can be improved and, in the process, getting "more bang" for the dollar.

The recommendations which follow can clearly put you and your firm on the right path to reducing or eliminating inefficient sales activity. By instituting my recommendations you will in fact place your sales personnel in more legitimate face-to-face sales situations; thereby increasing the probability of making the sales. In today's highly competitive business environment, you simply cannot afford to have a sales strategy which has salespeople knocking on every door in hope of finding a prospect for their sales pitch. This method is too time consuming, costly, demoralizing, and, most important, ineffective. By approaching sales opportunities with carefully predetermined plan, you are in effect cutting through all the fat which weighs down most sales programs. Your effort must be concentrated on those prospects which have shown a genuine interest and/or need for your product or service.

In this book, you will learn how to identify "hot" prospects and how to correctly measure the level of urgency. I will show you how to determine whether it is more feasible to maintain company sales personnel or hire an outside commissioned sales agent. You will learn the elements of an effective selling program. Unless you know what they are, you have a task similar to driving cross-country without a roadmap.

To help eliminate useless wheel-spinning, I will provide you with some effective methods of finding interested prospects for your product. If you have decided to use an independent agent, I will suggest ways to find and select this person. I will also go into how to get the most cooperation from agents to enhance the sale of your product.

Probably the most important element of a successful sales program is the people it hires and trains to ultimately make it happen! Just why is it some companies never seem to hire the best personnel? Once you learn the fundamentals you, too, can hire and retain good salespeople who will help your company grow and prosper. Just as important is the management of the salesforce. The sales manager must walk a fine line between the best interests of his employer and the people he supervises. He must be able to understand each personality and carefully cultivate the salesperson, encouraging him to produce to his individual peak potential.

My recommendations also include how your firm can tap the vast potential of a sound telemarketing program to reduce waste and inefficiency in your sales program. Also included are ideas on how sales meetings can be improved to get more bang for the dollar.

Overall I have attempted to provide you with enough insight into what it takes to make any sales effort run more efficiently, while reducing the amount of wasted resources. Moreover, I have provided areas of focus which should serve as starting points for re-evaluating your sales program. The results of your evaluation might suggest implementation of either some, or all, of my recommendations. The degree of your present efficiency will, in the final analysis, determine what new program, if any, should be instituted.

The underlying purpose of this book is to increase the awareness of management of the need to monitor sales activities carefully, constantly considering new ways to increase the level of efficiency of any sales program. I would very much appreciate your feedback on this book and on the results of any suggestions which you have implemented in your selling program. You can write to me in care of this publisher.

PART ONE

THE ECONOMICS OF SELLING

THE ECONOMICS OF SELLING

Increasing sales efficiency is a task which requires you to take two steps forward, followed by one step backwards. All new business obtained, given the same yearly volume, cannot be considered equal.

Far too many sales executives look only at the surface of their sales results believing that by increasing the customer base they are in fact increasing sales. But on closer inspection you can see that this can be most deceiving. For example, you may be calling on an account who may require more time to produce the same level of revenue as some of your other accounts, even though these accounts may require less of your time; or perhaps after calculating your cost you may find that an account's slow payment of your bills can well be eating away into your profits.

Therefore, it may sometimes be worth your while to accept less business from a given customer to reduce your cost of doing business and in the process increase the effectiveness of the sales effort.

I can recall one large chain which always deliberately waited to pay their bills. None of the suppliers complained too loudly because of the amount of business the company generated. Suppliers were reluctant to raise their prices, in fact they lowered them. I can say with a fair amount of confidence that few if any of these suppliers knew the true cost of doing business with this chain.

The Product Sales Report

The product sales report is the key to understanding and managing product sales. The fundamental ingredient in starting to cut away the fat from your sales program is knowing your cost of selling. Cost should be itemized, constantly revised, scrutinized, and weighed against the industry norm to gauge your performance against your competition. By itemizing costs, you can quickly spot trends which are emerging and react accordingly before they eat away at profits. In addition, keeping detailed product sales reports, with monthly updates, will assist you in tracking the acceptance and profitability of your product. If demand is decreasing, you can prepare for the product's withdrawal from the market before it becomes a burden to your program. When analyzing the sales of the product in units, remember that a few bad months are not a solid reason for withdrawing the product from the market. Factors which can have an adverse affect on sales can include: long periods of bad weather, a weak economy, and negative press, to mention just a few. Develop sales criteria based on a much larger picture, including considerations such as season, economic conditions, and industry trends. Only then can you make a correct assessment. Sales reports can also alert you to unexpected possibilities. For example, if your unit sales are rising when other competitors are dropping, is there another use for your product you are not aware of? If so, determine what it is and alter your selling angle to maximize the opportunity.

Contribution Accounting

Contribution accounting allows you to determine the fixed cost of each product or service. This method allows you to determine which product is contributing revenue and how much revenue in excess of cost. It is done as follows:

1. Determine income generated by the measured unit (product or service).

2. Subtract all variable expenses and cost, such as direct labor, direct materials, sales cost, etc.

By subtracting all variable costs and, in some instances, some fixed costs from the total income generated by the product or service, you have now determined the amount of revenue this unit generates. It can then be compared to other units and a determination can be made as to what strategy will be pursued for each unit, i.e., will the unit be phased out, will selling be increased, or will selling activities regarding this unit remain the same?

Once you have determined the individual unit cost and have made an evaluation of the role of each unit, you are ready to continue the evaluation process by reviewing other areas of the sales function vital to increasing the return on your selling investment.

Increasing Sales Effectiveness

Because the purpose of your sales effort is to get your product or service to the end-user, you have one important non-traditional middleman to deal with, the salesperson. You will find that the 80/20 rule applies here:

- 20% of your sales force produces 80% of your volume.
- 20% of your customers produce 80% of your volume.

- 20% of your products produce 80% of your volume.
- 20% of your time is spent effectively, and 80% is ineffective or wasted.

It has often been said, "If you are not part of the solution then you are the problem!" This idea applies to sales people who spend an increasing amount of time on non-selling activities, a practice which leads to nothing more than increased cost. Have your sales people keep a diary for one whole week at fifteen minute intervals and see how much time is spent driving, waiting, talking on the telephone, and how little time is actually spent on sales presentations. To pursue this line of thought further, figure the hypothetical cost of a salesperson. Take someone making a realistic base salary of $25,000 per year, add bonus and/or commissions, travel expenses, entertainment and miscellaneous expenses.

SALARY	$25,000
BONUS/COMMISSION	$ 2,500
TRAVEL	$10,000
ENTERTAINMENT	$ 3,750
MISCELLANEOUS EXPENSES	$ 475
	$41,725 total cost of salesperson per year

There are approximately 2,000 working hours in a calendar year, and remember the 80/20 rule.

2,000 x .20 = 400 selling hours per year,

$$\frac{\$41,725}{400} = \$104.31 \text{ per selling hour}$$

Keep in mind that I have added nothing for the cost of insurance benefits, taxes, etc. You can readily see that it is very important to get the most bang for your dollar and that good supervision of the sales force is the foundation of a sound sales effort.

Preparing a call-frequency schedule is the first major task the salesperson and his supervisor must accomplish in order to enhance the chances for reaching the full potential of the territory. An acceptable average number of calls per day must be established for the assigned territory, and specified objectives upon which the salesperson will be evaluated must be set for each call.

The accounts in the assigned territory should be divided into three groups, with the most profitable included in the first group, the intermediate accounts in the second group, and the least profitable in the last group. Once the classification of accounts is complete, you must then determine what percentage of time should be spent on each type, for example:

Classifications	Number of Accounts	Amount of Time Spent
1	20	43%
2	60	37%
3	20	20%
	100	100%

To determine specifically what percentage of time should be allocated to each type, you must do the following calculations:

52 weeks per year

 2 minus vacation time

50 working weeks available (including holidays)

50 weeks x 5 days = 250 working days.

Assuming that there are 250 working days, that the sales-person can make 8 calls per day given the nature of his concentrated territory with no overnight travel, and that you would like the salesperson to canvass one day per week, we can draw the following conclusions:

50 weeks x 1 day to canvass = 50 days per year

50 x 8 calls per day = 400 canvass calls per year

5 (days) x 8 (sales calls) x 50 (weeks) = 2,000 total calls per year available which leads us to

Classification	Number of Accounts	Time Spent	Allotment of Calls
1	20	43%	688
2	60	37%	592
3	20	20%	320
		canvass calls	400
			2,000

The salesperson now has workable guidelines to schedule the workload not only on a weekly basis, but for the months ahead as well. The variables which can cause some changes in strategy are the number of prospects available, heavy time demand by some customers, and working away from assigned territory. Still, all in all, this type of planning between salesperson and immediate supervisor is essential for productive selling.

There are other methods of increasing sales effectiveness while costs remain relatively constant. For example, you can increase the total number of sales calls per year, however, you must pay close attention to the effectiveness of someone who is able to increase the number of calls. As always you must look beyond the surface to correctly assess the impact of the increased activity. If you discover that the closing ratio for this person has in fact dropped from 10% to 7%, while his business expenses increased because he visited more prospects, you can easily come to the conclusion that sales quality has been replaced by sheer quantity. The consequence in the long run will probably be increased sales volume with declining profitability, which if left unchecked will erode your profits and leave you weak, vulnerable and ready to belly up if a major crisis beyond your control should occur.

Another method of increasing effectiveness is to increase the sales revenue per unit. This can be done by reducing the cost necessary to produce the product you sell, or the cost of materials used to perform a service. The salesforce should always make it their business to observe the competition and snoop around for any activity that can assist their firm in becoming more competitive. Management must encourage such observation by asking about it during regular reporting cycles and offering bonuses for good, solid, useful information. Then spread the word when bonuses are earned so that other members of the salesforce will know you mean business.

Also, increasing the percentage of closings will increase productivity while keeping costs in check. Increasing the closing ratio from 1 to 10, to 1 to 9, out of 400 canvass calls can add up to 4 new accounts per year per salesperson.

Prospect Identification

Often the sales manager has a better understanding of the accounts in his assigned area than a salesperson new to the territory would have. The manager can orient the salesperson, thus eliminating much wasted time the new salesperson would otherwise have to go through to familiarize himself with the accounts. Pointing out what types of business to go after, or any other unique situation unfamiliar to the salesperson, can assist in making the selling effort more profitable.

There are various methods of identifying potential prospects such as demographic data, industry classifications, location,

size, etc. A customer profile should be compiled of high potential
accounts either at the district office or at the field level. A
comparison should then be made to existing customers to identify
similar traits and possible areas to be emphasized when making the
sales presentation. In addition, the customer profile provides
leads to the industries where the sales effort should be concentrated. The profile can also suggest the relative potential of
sales territories and is an invaluable aid in making projections
for future personnel needs as well as sales and marketing expenditures.

Classification of Prospects

Once the prospects have been identified, you must now dissect
each individual prospect according to the various elements which
make this account unique. Classification of the prospects includes everything from identifying the influential person who can
authorize purchases to evaluating the potential amount of products
used, which your firm can supply. During this stage a plan should
be formulated to increase the prospect's awareness level of your
firm and what your firm can do for the prospect.

Payback

Once you have determined the cost of each salesperson you can review each territory and analyze the feasibility of each situation on its own merit. Let's go back to the salesperson we earlier calculated to cost $41,725 to maintain. We total up the sales figures and come up with a grand total of $430,000 for the past year. The average return on the widgets sold is 7%. Is this salesperson contributing to the firm or is he a liability?

$$\$430,000 \times (.07) = \$30,000 \text{ (Profit contributed by salesperson)}$$

$$\underline{\$41,725} \text{ (Cost of operating territory)}$$

$$(\$11,725) \text{ (Deficit contribution)}$$

As you can see, this is an area for concern. Can this be turned around? Is this territory big enough to support a company salesperson, or are you better off going through a commissioned agent? Does this territory have too many travel expenses? Can the territory be divided among existing territories? These are the kinds of questions which must be addressed and answered. In short, given this salesperson assigned to this territory, how much sales revenue must he generate to break even?

$$BE = \frac{\$41,725}{(.07)} \quad \begin{array}{l} \text{(Cost of salesperson)} \\ \text{(gross profit margin)} \end{array}$$

BE = \$596,071 (total gross sales needed in territory
to break even)

$596,071 (break even point)

- 430,000 (actual gross sales)

($166,071) (amount of deficit generated by territory)

This salesperson must increase his sales by $166,071 only to break even! Can he do it? Does the territory have the potential? Are your products competitive enough? Management must be truthful with itself.

I once did some work for a company who thought they had a product comparable to its competition. However, when the sales-peolple went out to canvass for new customers, they met with quite a bit of stiff resistance. Consequently, the firm generally had its greatest success in accounts which were not desired by the competition. The salesforce were aware of the situation they were up against, but could not honestly tell management because the latter were convinced they had a great product. As a result there was a great deal of turnover within the salesforce, and management was convinced that it was impossible to hire good sales talent.

Here is another example. A large industrial concern with many divisions decided, in one of the divisions, that since they had had their best year ever, they would change the minimum order quantities the following year. They were to set the pace for that segment of the industry! The salesforce who were canvassing for new business quickly realized the problem at hand when the minimum order quantity tripled. Existing customers did not mind too much because of the large quantities they used, but new customers could not often meet the minimum order. By the end of the selling season, because business did not grow at the "projected" growth rate, the division was merged with another division. The senior people were "shocked" when told that the new order quantities were unacceptable even for this well-known firm. They went from their best sales year to the worst ever, all because management would not listen, investigate, and react intelligently. I urge decision makers not to make decisions on logic that is dated. This is one weakness I have seen consistently in organizations of all different sizes. "When I was out in the field . . ." is often a pretext to an outdated war story.

Additional Points

Some other cost factors which must be considered and watched are:

1. Do you have too many sales people? Can some areas be consolidated without losing effectiveness?

2. Are salaries truly based on results or dependent upon the length of time the salesperson has been with the company? This is an area where I have seen great injustices done to good producers. Salaries not based on merit are a great way to lose good people. Does your firm offer compensation competitive with the industry?

3. Is your firm providing enough incentive for the salesforce? Is advancement too easy or unattainable?

4. Are your selling approaches allowing you to maximize the resources you have available?

Customer Service

As I have pointed out, most salesforces just do not spend enough time selling. It is most important that sales management create an atmosphere where there is a reduction of clerical function wherever possible to allow the salesperson maximum time for selling. Such things as writing orders, handling complaints, assisting information seekers, and writing reports of claims should be handled by the customer service department. Do not underestimate the importance of having very capable people in this function, or you will see in record time how quickly you lose customers out of frustration.

Simple matters like messages that are not relayed, and unanswered questions which may be of little importance to the staff but significant to the customer, can and will create a lot of bad feeling. Often a prospect may call in -- perhaps someone a salesperson has called on repeatedly to gain a foothold in his business -- but once coming in contact with the customer service people the customer has second thoughts about doing business with the firm. Such things as attitude problems, an implied lack of professionalism, problems placing orders, lack of support for the salesperson, etc., can be devastating to your company's image.

If your business is one that deals with highly technical products, a special centralized inquiry-handling center staffed with the appropriate personnel can be a real advantage. They can relay information to the salesperson for a visit and perhaps lead to additional sales.

Another suggestion for utilizing customer service would be to place minimum order quantities for a personal call. This would reduce the cost of selling, while the salesperson could spend more time selling. These inside sales people should be trained in sales techniques ranging from upgrading orders to substituting orders or dealing with stockouts. Once a customer is familiar with your products and company, the selling becomes an easier task.

While some may think of customer service as an additional unnecessary cost, I urge you to consider the implications of customer dissatisfaction.

Company Cars

Unless all your sales activities are handled from the home office, there is a good chance that your firm provides company cars. This can chew away at profits if left unchecked. Here are some tips to assist you in getting costs under control.

SIZE OF CARS: The time is long overdue to switch to subcompact cars. With costs escalating on everything from fuel to tires, there simply is no reason not to do so.

OPERATING CONDITION: A badly running car absorbs gas like a sponge. Develop a sound maintenance program with a local service station.

INCENTIVES: Instituting prizes for the best fuel economy would be a good incentive to instill good driving habits. Have someone come in to give a lecture on defensive driving, along with tips on saving fuel and repair costs.

JUSTIFY NEED: Do a complete review and justify that everyone who has a company car really does need it to perform his job. Can consolidating territories or developing a solid telemarketing program reduce the number of cars in your fleet?

EXPENSE REPORTS: Set solid guidelines for reimbursable expenses and do not waver. Lodging and meal allowances are the type of expenses which must be periodically reviewed to keep abreast of escalating costs.

- Use discounts whenever possible.
- Remember that proper planning before trips reduces the amount of wasted expenditures later on.
- And, most important, monitor expense reports and ask questions about unexplained charges.

Summary

The first order of business when evaluating a selling program is to know exactly what your costs are. By familiarizing yourself with all the elements of the fixed and variable costs involved in the course of running your business, you are in a position to accurately evaluate current efficiency, and strategically plan new tactics for increased efficiency.

By carefully analyzing the selling program, non-productive activities can be identified and specific areas where improvements can lead to increased efficiency can be discovered. Scrutinizing costs of sales territories and comparing them with generated volume can point out problem areas which require attention. Sales supervisors play an important role in helping to shape sales productivity by assisting in planning the workload and coaching the salesperson into peak performance, monitoring sales activities, and providing feedback on a constant basis.

Do not underestimate the importance of a sound customer service program to your total sales effort. Do not stick your deadwood or any other undesirables in customer service or you will soon live to regret it.

Finally, take a long hard look at your fleet of company cars or your reimbursement policy for the use of personal cars. Always look into methods of reducing these expenses, and closely monitor and question any unexplained charges. Remember that a thriving business is a business that carefully controls costs.

PART TWO

THE SALES STAFF

I. THE INTERVIEWING, HIRING, AND TRAINING OF SALES PERSONNEL

I am amazed by the number of firms who have never taken the time to calculate the actual cost of employee turnover! There is little difference in who terminated the employment, either way it is costly. Management can greatly enhance the final outcome of employee turnover by reducing faulty hiring. We can again cite the 80/20 rule in hiring salesmen: 80% of those hired will not stand a chance of performing satisfactorily for any prolonged period of time, whether it's because they have little or no sales ability or they are selling the wrong product for their given "talent". What are some of the consequences to first level sales management of turnover?

1. Turnover puts constraints on the firm's ability to compete in the marketplace.
2. It inhibits the ability to take advantage of spot oppor-tunities.
3. It does not allow utilization of full potential of first level supervision.

Your firm's ability to hire the right sales personnel will play an integral part in the success of your selling effort.

Consequently, it is imperative that the selection process be handled in the most efficient manner if it is to produce the desired results.

Before the interview process begins, a complete and thorough description of duties and responsibilities of specific positions should be written. This provides all who will take part in choosing the candidate with a complete guide on which to base their opinions.

Make sure to ask specific questions to determine if the qualities desired are found in a candidate. Also consider the following:

- Do not allow the candidate to control the interview. This will only eat away at your time, drag out the interview and prevent you from asking the pointed questions required.
- What does the candidate know about your firm? Why is he looking for another job?
- Does he have a trait which will turn off customers during the presentation?

- Make sure there are interruptions during the interview. This will occur during sales calls. Observe the candidate.

- Is the candidate over-aggressive to the point where it can turn off your customers?

Let's examine some of the reasons why managers have difficulty in hiring good sales talent.

1. One major problem is weak interviewing skills. Interviewing skills simply cannot be gained by reading some books. It would be useful to attend a seminar/workshop on personnel function.

2. Managers often do not get enough useful information about applicants to make a proper evaluation.

3. When more than one manager interviews the applicant there is often too much information overlap to make the most of two opinions.

4. Managers sometimes enter interviews with preconceived ideas as to what type of applicant will be successful.

5. Managers sometimes make the mistake of allowing one attribute to overshadow all other factors.

In determining the requirements that will make an applicant qualified for further consideration, the company must include in its statement of duties and responsibilities such aspects as:

- The importance of first-call closing
- The ability to work independently and the ability to plan a work schedule
- The ability to work with and provide detailed work
- The ability to work well with other company personnel
- The drive required to carry out company policy
- The ability to effectively communicate with both customers and company personnel
- The ability to make decisions on his own

Once the pre-screening has been completed and the second round of interviews has begun, more detailed questions must be asked in order to delve deeper into the applicant's work history. If you can come up with a complete history of experiences and events, it can provide a pretty good indicator of what to expect. Here are some general guidelines to consider when hiring either a sales representative or an outside agent:

A. Salary: The amount that will be provided and at what intervals

B. Draw: How it is to be computed, the liability of the person receiving it and rights of company to alter/terminate it

C. Bonus: The criteria for determining the amount

D. Commission: The rate at which it will be paid, the split with other personnel provisions

E. Expenses: Specific types which are eligible for reimbursement, the maximum amount, if applicable, and the documentation required

F. Territory: Bounderies, exclusivity, and crossing into someone else' territory bounderies

G. Duties: All duties and responsibilities required of sales personnel

H. Employment Conditions: The contract/agreement between employee/employer. The notice required by either party to terminate relationship. Remember never to offer guarantees of any kind. It will only come back to haunt you.

Our society has "promoted" certain myths about job performance in certain groups that I would like to dispel:

1. Under 40 and over 40: There is no evidence of significant differences in performance levels between these groups, and it is well to remember that the over 40's group will continue to increase as the baby-boomers reach middle age.

2. Men versus Women: There is no difference in performance between the sexes, even the traditionally male industries have reported outstanding performances by women.

3. Black versus White: Blacks have performed as well as whites and turnover is the same.

4. Experience versus Inexperience: Once the inexperienced person receives training and supervision his chances for success are just as good as they are for the experienced one. I must caution you on the "experienced" applicant. There are far too many people working just well enough to avoid dismissal, but who are far from performing on the outstanding level. Therefore, the value of experience is relative.

Training

Once you have selected one of the applicants, you must now provide him with the best possible training and supervision, which will allow him to make positive contributions to the sales program. Teaching does not necessarily imply learning. Learning, the transfer of skills, facts, or attitudes by one person to another, can be facilitated in the following ways:[1]

1. Doing may be the best way of learning. (While lecturing is a most popular method of training, it is probably the least effective teaching method).
2. Holding discussions with trainees regarding their experiences is a most effective method of learning.
3. Demonstration, followed by direct participation of traines will re-enforce learning.

We have all known for sometime that we forget much of what we have read and learned in school. It is generally expected that we can remember

    5 to 10 percent of non-illustrated lectures,

    30 to 50 percent of visual presentations,

    50 to 70 percent of role-playing demonstrations,

and

    70 to 90 percent of early experience in actual use of learning.

To state it another way, workers learn 10 percent of what they hear, 30 percent of what they see, 50 percent of what they hear and see, but 90 percent of what they year, see and do.

You can readily see why a well-planned training program is a must. The sink or swim method is not only too costly but can lead to a frustrated trainee.

What are some of the elements of a sound training program? Like any other business matter, it requires some thoughtful preplanning with consideration given to the following:

1. Select the job of the typical salesman in your organization and prepare a job description of his duties.

2. Decide what method of training shall be employed in the presentation of each area of subject matter.

3. Assign responsibility to any individuals who are to assist in the presentation of the sales training program.

4. Outline the program and prepare materials for each type of training in the program.

5. Provide for further training through correspondence, refresher courses, or sales meetings.

6. Get the approval of all your assistants, whom you expect to help you with this training.

7. Arrange a program whereby the results of sales training can be measured.

8. Follow up on your sales training, and find out how salespeople are performing on the job, from the point of view of customers or distributors.

The training instructor's job is to gain the interest and confidence of the participants; and then, understanding what they know and what he should teach next, to present the lessons attractively, logically and simply. The instructor must follow a basic four-step process to enhance learning.

I. Prepare the learner:

- Put him at ease.
- Describe the job and find out what he already knows about it.
- Get him interested in learning the job.
- Put him in the right location for his present sales abilities.

II. Present the operation:

- Tell, show, and illustrate one important step at a time. Tell him WHY.
- Stress each key point -- do's and dont's.
- Instruct clearly, completely, and patiently, but not more than he can master at one time.

- Answer questions, clarify.

III. Try out performance:
- Have the trainee do the job. Correct errors.
- Have him explain each key point to you as he does the job again.
- Make sure he understands.
- Continue until you know he knows.

IV. Follow-up:
- Put the trainee on his own. Designate to whom he should go for help.
- Check frequently. Encourage questions.
- Begin normal supervision and controls.

Where Learning Takes Place Best

HOME OFFICE

Home office training has the advantage of placing a prospective sales representative near you and your assistants so that he can spend regular periods with you, sit in on company meetings, and pick up company information, including engineering practices which cannot be found elsewhere.

AT THE PLANT

Plant experience is especially useful for learning to sell industrial goods. The sales representative for heavy and light equipment -- often a graduate engineer -- needs to know how a machine is put together, how it can be adapted to slightly different operating conditions and slightly different uses. He will be talking to technical shop people in the plants of his customers. There is simply no better method of gaining the necessary knowledge and the confidence that goes with it.

TRAINING ON THE ROAD

If the new salesman has sufficient prior experience and has a good understanding of your product line, policies, and company, you may decide to put him on the road immediately. Usually, however, you will want him to have the close supervision and guiding hand of one of your experienced salesmen, supervisors, or officers. In this type of situation, let me add the following:

1. When one of two men is doing the selling, it is best that the other remain silent.
2. The boss should never "take over" in the middle of a selling job that the salesman is trying to do.

The following is a checklist of suggested subjects to be covered during the orientation/training period:

- Introduction of new company officers
- Company problems - old and new
- Analysis of general business conditions
- Changes in sales policies
- Explanation of changes in established lines
- New price schedules
- Appraisal of market conditions
- Analysis of competing products
- Review of selling problems
- Product and sales plans for the future
- Presentations of model sales talks
- Discussion of paper work required of salesmen
- How to increase productive time of salesmen

Not only is it necessary to determine what subjects are to be discussed, but also who is to present them. Clearly, it is to the advantage of your business to have all your top assistants take part in such refresher meetings. It helps the salesmen and it benefits the executives as well.

Training Methods and Devices

You can achieve greater effectiveness in your sales training by the intelligent use of aids which make their appeal through the eye as well as the ear. In this way, you follow the established training principle of "show and tell". Let's review some of the tools which can be used effectively in any sales training program.[2]

TRAINING MANUALS: There are many firms which specialize in preparing sales training manuals.

INDUSTRIAL FILMS: There are numerous industrial films for just about any function and operation of a manufacturing company.

SOUND SLIDE FILMS: These can be used to tie in visual training more closely to your own business.

TAPE RECORDERS: After a salesman in training has given some thought to his presentation and possibly developed an outline of a proposed sales talk, it is often helpful for him to tape his talk so that he can hear what he sounds like.

VIDEO-TAPES: This is the most useful method in sales training. There are two types. (1) The video taken of one's own salesmen (for their own use primarily), and (2) the video that is taken of a sales meeting demonstration and immediately re-run.

ROLE-PLAYING: This method is successful between trainee and salesman, or between two salesmen.

RECORDS AND CASSETTES: There are various outstanding talks on sales methods, leadership development, and other sales training topics produced by manufacturers, trade associations, etc.

LIBRARY: Do not forget the resources of your local library. Ask about them, especially in the larger cities.

CHARTS AND DIAGRAMS: A large model of your organization chart will be useful to a new sales rep who wants to see what functions are performed and by whom.

PUBLICATIONS: While the salesman is in training he should be taught the value of scanning, if not reading, business publications covering general business conditions, your particular industry, and selling.

TRADE ASSOCIATIONS: Many national and regional trade associations offer courses in selling to the salesmen of member companies at a nominal cost.

EDUCATIONAL INSTITUTIONS: Many state and city universities, and private ones, offer evening classes for adults, including businessmen and their employees.

Dealing with Poor Performance

After you have provided a salesman with the best training and supervision possible, there will come a time when you will have to come to grips with the poor performance of some employees. You should first sit down with the employee to discuss the poor performance. At times, you might need the assistance of others to provide counseling for physical or mental conditions, alcohol or drug abuse, or other personal problems. If the employee does not understand exactly what must be done to bring performance to an acceptable level, you should tell him. Immediately after any discussion with the employee, you should take a few minutes and make a dated memo for the file (with a copy for the employee), which documents the matters discussed and any assistance offered.

If the employee continues to produce unacceptable work in at least one critical element of the job, or if at the end, the performance is unacceptable, give the employee a reasonable time to show that he can do the critical element(s). The time required depends on the employee's job. Typically, this can vary from 30 to 90 days.

During this period the employer must assist the employee to reach acceptable performance in any appropriate way, such as classroom or informal training, counseling, intensive coaching, etc. You should exercise close supervision over the employee and provide frequent oral feedback on work produced. Again, note for the record, with a copy to the employee, each thing done and when. However, written notes need not be sent for each observation to the employee. Records should be kept, but sent to the employee only at reasonable intervals.

At the end of the 30 to 90 day period of time, the employee must have demonstrated whether or not he can do the work at an acceptable level. The employer must then decide what to do next. If the employee has reached acceptable performance levels, there is no need for any further action except to keep providing feedback and encouragement to the employee. If the employee is still performing unacceptably, you must take some action, at the very least, reassigning the employee out of the job which he clearly has shown he cannot perform, or finally, terminating the employee.

Drugs and Alcoholism in the Workplace

Prior to the 1940's, an employee with an alcohol problem, as shown by poor job performance, was usually seen as weak or immoral, with public mores dictating corporate attitudes. Punitive measures centering around medical treatment or actual dismissal were the pattern, but these approaches often hurt the individual and were costly to the company, which lost an experienced employee in whom they had an investment.

The drug scene of the late sixties and early seventies became increasingly visible in the workplace.[3] Initially industry's position regarding drug abuse among its employees was denial. Retaliatory, punitive measures, based on disapproval, often followed the denial phase. Some screening and policing efforts, including random urinalysis and the hiring of undercover agents, were undertaken, and the employee who was obviously using or selling drugs was often dismissed immediately. The possible legal issues and the difficulty in substantiating accusations caused some corporations to refrain from acting at all except in the most obvious cases.

Industry has in some cases followed the Department of Defense program of education, rehabilitation, and treatment to combat both the lost productivity of its personnel and the high social cost. The military, like the private sector, generally emphasizes recognition of problems, intervention, referral, treatment, and rehabilitation. These are continuing efforts, with emphasis on assessing, determining, detecting drug abuse, and drug trafficking; education and training; treatment and counseling; discipline and discharge where necessary and appropriate; prohibiting possession, use and sales of drug paraphernalia, and working collaboratively with national alcohol and drug abuse prevention programs.

The fact that most businesses have not utilized community treatment alternatives may result from:

1. a lack of kowledge concerning resources available,
2. a desire to keep "hidden" internal problems or substance--abusing employees,
3. fear of law enforcement requirements or actions,
4. concern that they will be asked by agencies to provide additional financial assistance or hire rehabilitated clients, and

5.   inappropriate personnel and treatment options available for
      the employed drug abuser.

What are some of the reasons that someone will turn to drugs
or alcohol?   There are many; most reasons are usually stress
related.   It can run from failure to obtain promotion, pressures
of competition both external and internal, deadline pressures, and
fear of failure -- or success.   An employer must try to help an
employee through such crises with whatever resources are at his
disposal, because this will not only reaffirm the commitment to the
employee, but also show other employees the concern the company has
for its workforce.   This in turn can manifest itself in renewed
employee dedication.

Here are some sources which can provide assistance in dealing
with employee drug abuse:

- The National Association of Alcoholism Treatment Programs
  in Irving, California -- (also offers help with drug abuse
  problems)
- The drug crisis Hot Line 1-800-COCAINE.
- The local office of the American Medical Association.
- Your local Public Health Service.

Summary

Since the salesman is an integral part of the selling program, the ability to hire good personnel is of monumental importance. Those responsible for the interviewing and hiring of new personnel must have a clear understanding of the interviewing process and a complete and thorough description of duties and responsibilities of the job, to insure the hiring of the best possible candidate.

The new employee must now be the recipient of the best possible training his employer can provide. The trainer must gain the interest and confidence of the participants if he is to be an effective instructor. For best results, the most effective learning process should have the trainee hear, see and do the critical parts of his future responsibilities. Moreover, the use of audiovisuals can greatly enhance learning effectiveness.

Bad employee performance should be dealt with in a clear, concise, and thorough manner, keeping the employee informed of what is expected and the consequences likely to occur if no improvement is forthcoming.

Drug abuse in the workplace should be dealt with early. To improve the chances of recovery, seek professional help immediately. Keep detailed records of events during crises, take a firm stand on treatment requirements and clearly spell out the consequences of resistance, i.e., loss of job.

II. Sales Management

Show me a company which is weak and inefficient in selling its product or service, and I will show you a terminally ill company. A closer look at the financial reports of just about all companies which have gone out of business will reveal the declining trend for several years prior to the final curtain. While strong sales volume alone will not ensure a healthy prosperous company, it can certainly have a great impact on a firm's success and tend to help overcome other weaknesses.

Good sales programs start with management's understanding, and ability to develop, solid marketing and sales programs which will allow their product the maximum opportunity to sell in the market place. The most popular theme followed today is built around the "marketing concept", which essentially says, to iden-tify and satisfy customer needs at a profit. Consequently, all company policies and activities should be predicated on satisfying customer need. Also profitable sales volume is a better goal than maximum sales volume.

A sound strategy implies that a business cannot be all things to all people and must analyze its markets and its own capabilities to focus on a target market it can best serve. What are some of the factors which should be considered in market planning?

1. Determine the needs of the customer (a good place to start can be the present customer base you now serve).[4]

2. Analzye your own competitive advantages, and those of the competition as well.

3. Select specific markets to serve.

4. Determine how to satisfy those needs.

MARKET SEGMENTATION

Concentrating the sales and marketing effort on one, or a few segments, is also the basis of a sound strategy. Some of the bases for segmentation are:

1. Geographic: Cultivating a group of customers in a given geographical territory before expanding into other territories.

2. Product: Maximizing the existing product(s) potential before introducing new products.

3. Customer: identifying and promoting to those groups of people most likely to buy the products. In other words, selling to the heavy users before trying to develop new users.

There are four key marketing decision areas in a marketing and sales program -- sometimes referred to as "the four P's". They are Product and Services, Promotion, Pricing, and Physical Distribution.

PRODUCTS AND SERVICES: An effective strategy might include concentrating all efforts on a small product line, or developing a specialized product or service.

PROMOTION: A determination must include decisions on advertising, salesmanship, and any other pertinent promotional activity.   A strong selling effort is necessary for those firms that are unable to advertise heavily.   Do not overlook good yellow page advertising if your business is in the retail end, and direct mail is an effective low-cost medium of advertising.   More on this later.

PRICE: The determination of price levels and/or pricing policies will have significant impact on total revenue.   Higher prices usually lead to low sales volume and vice versa.

PHYSICAL DISTRIBUTION: The manufacturer and wholesaler/distributor must decide how to distribute their product working either by using the company facilities or established distributors.   A determination must be made once having weighed all the ramifications.

In the course of setting up marketing and sales strategy, some provisions must be set forth to evaluate actual performance against some pre-determined standard. Sound data on industry trends and past performance provide the basis for judging present performance. Some of the factors to be considered are the following:

1. Is the company doing all it can to provide customers with what they want?
2. Is the customer satisfied enough with your company's product to return again?
3. Can your customer easily find what he wants at a competitive price elsewhere?

There are various directories which offer valuable information to help you keep abreast of the variety of services and products in today's complex marketplace to further enhance the planning function. Some of the directories which can assist you in finding such information include:

- Fur Source Directory
- Womens & Children Wear & Association Buyers, Nationwide Directory

- Electrical Wholesale Distributors
- Thomas Grocery Register
- Food Service Distributor

The above are only a small sampling of the directories available. Other references I urge you to inspect when making projections are the various government reports and publications such as:

- Bureau of the Census Catalog: lists all publications issued by the Bureau of Census
- Directory of Federal Statistics (for local areas): gives detailed table descriptions of subjects for almost all types of areas.
- Measuring Markets: A guide to the use of Federal and State statistical data
- Statistical Abstract of the United States: a comprehensive book on the social, economic, and governmental characteristics of the United States

    . . . this is just a small sample of the numerous kinds of information available from the U.S. government which can assist you in making future projections. I have included more titles in Appendix B.

LEADERSHIP

After top management has plotted strategy, it is up to lower level management to implement those plans and make it happen. It is the job of lower level supervision to lead the salesforce into the market place. This person, usually a District Sales Manager, is the kingpin who is asked to gain the cooperation of the salesforce to attain the desired results. This manager will somehow mesh the goals of his company with the wants and desires of each individual salesman. He must be a

> Teacher, advisor, trainer, coach, counselor, supervisor, friend, confidant, mentor, instigator, innovator, creator, developer, disciplinarian, administrator, controller, politician, etc., etc., etc.

As you can readily see, a District Sales Manager must be different things to differnt people, and he must sometimes present different personalities to the same people in different situations. Hiring a District Sales Manager, or promoting someone to this position, is not a task to be taken lightly. The abilities of the candidate in such areas as leadership, and motivation of both management and non-management personnel must be determined and evaluated to project future performance. It has been found that to get maximum results and reduce turnover, sales representatives should be hired who are compatible with the management style of the person to whom they will report. Because management style will probably not change very much, hiring personnel which will fit in is the best bet. What is management style anyhow? It is reflected in the way a manager designs jobs, maintains daily working habits, defines methods of evalution, conducts verbal and written communications and structures the chain of command.

Let's not forget that most sales managers were sales reps at one time. They enjoy selling because they find it motivating and, like sales reps, they enjoy recognition for a job well done. Sales people like the act of accomplishing the goals and objectives set for them by management. A company that does not acknowledge a sales rep's good performance will suffer some loss of cohesiveness between company and sales rep. Acknowledgment comes through such acts as appropriate salary increases, bonuses for outstanding achievements, rings, awards and such.

The District Sales Manager is the company's eyes and ears in the marketplace. He will accompany the salesforce on calls, gauge customer receptiveness to your sales story and company literature, show sales reps how to sell in breadth, calling on various top executives in different departments to maximize opportunities. Given the large task to be performed by the District Sales Manager, it is equally important that he is guided by a talented second-line manager.

No matter at what level an employee is positioned in the organizational chart, a major cause of dissatisfaction is a poor interpersonal relationship with his boss. This can be critical in a sales environment where rejection is such a large part of the selling function. If the atmosphere in the workplace is on anything but firm ground, the selling effort by the given salesman can deteriorate to a point where he will either leave or become a prime candidate for termination.

Another area for concern is the perception of a proliferation of paperwork. The personality of someone who is willing to face rejection in three out of four sales calls is, I think you would have to agree, of a totally, different nature than that of someone who stays in an office day after day spending his time on admin- istrative functions. Sales people are notorious for hating paperwork. However, management must have access to valuable market information which will provide benchmarks as to how well its strategy is working, and how the competition is doing. A careful balance, somewhere in the middle of these two divergent needs, must be found.

DELEGATION OF AUTHORITY

In every example which I can think of, the difference between an effective versus a non-effective leader is the ability to delegate authority and supervise accordingly. A manager should possess the three "I"s -- initiative, interest, and imagination.[5] He must have the ability to start things and have enough drive to see them through to completion, without having to be reminded repeatedly of chores to be completed. Personality traits must be considered. A manager should have the ability to overcome opposition when the chips are down and have enough perserverance to get a job done.

Effective delegation starts with a clear understanding of what is to be expected from whom! To reduce the chance of confusion of all those involved, make sure the departments are coordinated when you spell out responsibilities.

KEEPING CONTROL

It is essential that matters are kept under control when you manage personnel. Delegating authority to subordinates and holding them accountable is one method of keeping control; keeping the lines of communications open, is another; this will in turn provide the feedback which will keep you informed. Periodic staff meetings should be a weekly event. At these meetings department heads can comment on their activities, accomplishments, and problems and you can ask questions to ensure that the listener understands you. Delegation can only be effective when you have good communication.

One of the prerequisites of successful delegation is the ability to give subordinates freedom to operate. By consistently correcting and/or suggesting how to perform a task you risk the chance of destroying their self-confidence. It is important to keep in mind that you should not measure subordinates by how they perform a particular task. What should be judged is the end result, not their methods. Generally speaking, no two people will react exactly the same way to a given situation; for this reason, methods cannot be standardized. Only when the person strays too far from company policy should he be brought back in line. This would be a good time to review exactly what company policy is. In the final analysis, if the subordinate does not run the department to your satisfaction and the shortcomings cannot be overcome, then it's time to replace the person.

METHODS FOR PRODUCTIVITY IMPROVEMENT

The best way to achieve a high degree of job performance is to provide employees with opportunities for personal growth, achievement, responsibility, recognition and reward. Money is the primary need and reward; a secondary need is company recognition of the employee's desire to do work, to assume responsibility, to achieve, and to succeed. When considering changes in creating a new quality of work-life atmosphere, move:[6]

FROM: Detailed job description with specific tasks and rigid instruction on how to do the work.
  TO: Flexible, diverse work assignment allowing self-regulation, variety and challenge
FROM: Structured chain of command with managers making decisions and supervisors bossing
  TO: Worker involvement in planning, decision making, and operating procedure
FROM: Hierarchic channels of communication
  TO: Direct, fast two-way communications

FROM: Limited on the job instruction

  TO: Advanced training, educational and career development opportunities

FROM: Job specialization in one task

  TO: Leeway allowed for every employee to complete many tasks by crossing lines of specialization

FROM: Obscure, irregular job evaluations

  TO: Objective job performance standards with measures fairly administered

The key to achieving improved profit goals is to make jobs more interesting and provide rewards through quality of work-life techniques and procedures.

FLEXIBLE BENEFITS

Compensation costs, salaries, wages and benefits, are a large and increasing part of operating expenses yet productivity can decline among employees who get more pay and benefits. Ironically, not all employee motivation and productivity problems are solved by pay raises and promotions. It is not necessary to make pay adjustments beyond a fair industry-wide marketplace level. Employees are most productive when fair pay is tied to performance.

The tailoring of benefits to satisfy specific needs is part of the quality of work-life technique. Unwanted employee turnover and related recruiting, hiring, and training costs can be avoided by shifting these costs from developing new employees to keeping experienced employees. You can motivate an employee to increase productivity by providing opportunities for career development; thus, at the same time, you have improved the worker's skills and shown recognition of worker's value and aspirations. Such a benefit is practical because

1. It probably costs less than worker's unrest, diminished productivity, and

2. It is probably less costly than a comparable pay increase.

Age, education, job experience, job fulfillment, marital status, and family size are considerations that will determine the utility and attractiveness of a benefit. Different benefits appeal to different people. Everyone's needs are different. A younger employee might be motivated by having use of a company car. An older person may want more status like a title or a professional association membership. There are numerous possibilities, such as:

- Pre-tax thrift savings programs
- Recreational programs
- Discounts
- Scholarships
- Personal financial planning
- Loans
- Tuition refund
- Profit sharing
- Company car
- Personal expense accounts
- Parking privileges
- Legal assistance
- Extra vacation time
- Child care
- Job titles
- Professional or trade association memberships
- Travel
- Etc., etc., etc.

Using quality of work-life techniques to motivate and to reward employees can result in productivity gains. The ultimate goal, of course, is to achieve the maximum result from the least effort, the greatest profit for the least cost, the largest output from the smallest input. To work toward this goal, you've got to know how productive your company is.

MEASUREMENT OF PRODUCTIVITY

When all is said and done, you must determine how to measure the results of your efforts in increasing productivity. In the sales area a comparison of sales figures from one year to the next will indicate the degree of success achieved for your efforts. Input can also be measured by labor cost, hours worked, and number of employees. To be useful, measures must be simple and consistent. A basic and understandable method of productivity measurement is to divide total sales (output in dollars) by total compensation cost (input). Increases in compensation and prices are accounted for automatically; however, you must adjust for inflation. To compare productivity measures in different years, pick a base year and give it an index of 100. Then figure your ratio of compensation to sales and with that number calculate the index and compare the fluctuations of the indexes. For example, let's look at a hypothetical company with the following totals,

	19x0*	19x1	*base year
SALES	$1,000,000	$1,000,000	
TOTAL COMPENSATION	100,000	200,000	
RATIO	10 to 1	5 to 1	

As you can readily see the lower the sales to compensation ratio falls, the greater the levels of unproductive activity.

The indexes measure the productivity increases and decreases that indicate changes in your company's performance. You need these measures so that you

1. can set goals and priorities
2. know where you stand
3. are motivated by objective reasons, by numbers, not subjective feelings, and
4. have a common basis of communications with employees, bankers and consultants.

Companies must constantly monitor the productivity of their salesforce. Field supervisors should ideally spend 80% of their time working with the salesforce. For maximum results field supervisors should ideally have between seven to twelve full-time salesmen assigned to them. They will assist the sales reps in planning sales strategies, run their territories, and motivate them to perform up to their potential.

Equally important is the quality of sales generated by a given customer. Points to consider, as previously mentioned, are profit contribution, share of market, amount of time invested per call, return on assets managed, etc. An important factor in determining the degree of success attained will be the proper use of:

1. Long and short-term objectives
2. Weekly itinerary
3. Call reports
4. Forecasting of sales, classified by customers, products, and different markets if appropriate

By developing true distribution costs, management can readily determine what the contribution to profits are by region, district, sales territory, and type of customer. Productivity can also be isolated on a territory basis to determine the sales rep's contribution, such as cost per territory sales dollar, number of sales calls per order, miles traveled per call, new accounts opened per canvass call, etc.

MOTIVATION

Another major factor in the final outcome of your sales effort will be the ability to motivate the troops. This does not necessarily mean an expenditure of money. Motivating goes beyond increased volume, profits, and market share. It also means getting promotions off the ground, keeping expenses under control, and investing time wisely.

Management's approach and the salesperson's perception of their intention will be a significant determinant in the degree of success in motivating the salesforce. I have seen managers try to motivate by creating heavy peer pressure among the salesforce or "chewing out" those who fall behind sales quotas. I do not believe this type of mentality lends itself to the kind of environment which is necessary for good productive selling. The working environment must be such that the salesforce enjoy being part of it. Let's not forget the constant rejection that awaits your salesforce out in the field. By creating a pleasant environment, you are giving them the positive re-enforcement, or psychological stroking, which is strongly desired by most individuals throughout their lifetime.

Hiring the right type of person, one who will fit into your organization, is the first step towards motivating employees. If this means inviting an applicant back half-a-dozen times to get several opinions, so be it. The quality of first line supervisors will consequently play a major role in motivating the salesforce. Here are some of the major areas of responsibility a supervisor must concern himself with:

A.   He must set high but attainable goals for each one of his salesmen, and provide challenge and responsibility.

B.   He must provide frequent feedback on how well the salesman is doing and offer suggestions for improvement.

C.   He must develop a working relationship, personal concern, and sensitivity to the wants and needs of each salesman. This includes knowing when to be tough (but fair), and when to let them go at it on their own.

D.   He must develop a thorough knowledge of the salesman's job and must be familiar with events both inside and outside the company which may affect his people.

Motivation is one of the most potentially productive yet confusing responsibilities of sales managers today. To be effective at motivation requires not only understanding what it is, but being aware of the essential factors available to assist you.

Let's briefly review some factors which can improve performance:

PRIDE: Pride is a strong motivator. Once a person knows he is a member of a winning team, he is apt to perform at higher levels than ever before to maintain the status quo.

RECOGNITION: Here is another motivator which pays off handsomely. Ranging from a hand-written note from management expressing appreciation, to "salesman-of-the-year" awards, ongoing acts of recognition pay dividends.

ONE-TIME-AWARDS: These have to be powerful to reap maximum results, but they can mean permanent improvement in the performance of the entire salesforce.

BONES & COMMISSIONS: These ongoing programs can be converted to a permanent part of the salesman's compensation.

These motivational programs, used individually or in combination, can have the impact necessary to build the foundation of a solid sales organization.

ESSENTIALS OF PROBLEM SOLVING

What is a problem? It is a situation that presents difficulty or perplexity. Problems come in many shapes and sizes:

1. Something did not work as you expected, and you don't know why.
2. Something you need is unavailable and something must be found to take its place.
3. Employees are undermining a new program.
4. Your customers are not buying your product. What can you do to survive?
5. Customers are complaining. How do you handle their complaints?

A. Identifying the problem

Before a problem can be solved, you must first recognize that a problem exists.[7] Here is where problem-solving techniques become important. Do not become intimidated. Approach the problem as rationally as possible and remind yourself that every problem can be solved if approached appropriately. Fear can block your ability to think clearly. Instead:

1. Follow a systematic approach for finding solutions.

2. Realize that you can't predict everything.

3. Assume that your final decision is the best option at the time.

4. Realize that your solution might fail because situations change.

Once you recognize that a problem does exist, your next step is to identify it! First, you need to investigate how it happened. Probe for answers to questions like:

- Did something go wrong?
- Did something break down?
- Where did the unexpected results come from?
- Is something that worked once no longer working?

Then explore the nature of the problem.

- Is it people, operational, technical, etc.?
- Is it a product, service or a particular department?
- Is it tangible or intangible?

At this stage you must determine how significant the problem is. Is it significant enough that you need to take action, or can it be ignored?

- Is it disrupting operations?
- Is it affecting sales?
- Is it causing conflict among people?
- How often does it occur? Is it common?
- Is it affecting personnel and their productivity?
- Is it having an effect on customers, vendors, or any external people?

You should now start to narrow down the type of problem:

1. Has this problem occurred in the past? Review its history and make sure it does not happen again.
2. Is the problem a new one? Clear up the situation so that it won't become a recurrent problem.
3. Is this problem inevitably likely to occur again? Plan the actions you will take before the problem occurs.

The answers to all these questions will assist you in focusing on the true problem. To appropriately identify the problem and its causes, you must do some research to answer the questions fully. After you have gathered the information and reviewed it, you will have a better understanding of the problem and what the causes were.

Next, you should summarize the problem as briefly as possible, and list causes and effects. Then research a little further to determine:

- What has previously been done in regard to this problem
- What other companies have done
- What formal knowledge you need to acquire
- What has been learned from past experience
- What experts say about the problem

B. Obstacles to problem solving

Without realizing it many of us serve as the single biggest obstacle in solving a given problem. Why?

- Old habits
- Perceptions
- Assumptions

Here are some suggestions:

- Step back and take an objective look
- Do not procrastinate
- Curb your inclination to simply react, without planning
- Resist the temptation of rash, drastic solutions
- Avoid emotional responses; always try to be rational
- Realize that situations change
- Do not try to short-cut the problem-solving process

Now you are ready to check your understanding of the problem. You have isolated it, broken down its components, researched it, and narrowed it down. Study what you have done. Discuss it with your employees. Get their feedback. You might then decide to make some modifications in your thinking. Then summarize the problem as simply and thoroughly as possible.

C. Finding possible solutions

There are various methods for finding solutions to a problem. I recommend using several methods:

CONVENTIONAL ANALYSIS: This method is the one most commonly used. It requires:

1. A careful examination of each cause of the problem
2. A listing of all possible solutions based on knowledge and experience
3. A systematic check of all listed solutions with the research compiled on how the problem was handled by others

CALCULATED RISK: This method of problem solving is based upon hunches built on strong past experiences and facts.

BRAINSTORMING: This method features a free flow of ideas in an "anything goes" atmosphere. This can occur alone or in a group, although gathering a diverse group of people with different backgrounds is probably best. Once the problem is explained to group members, they are encouraged to contribute as many ideas as they can muster.

COMPARISON: This method involves comparing different facets of a problem with other problems which may or may not have similar characteristics.

D. Selecting the best solution

It is now time to go through your long list of solutions and eliminate those which would not work. List each of the remaining solutions separately on its own piece of paper. Then list all the advantages and disadvantages of each solution. Check each solution against the following criteria:

- Cost effectiveness
- Time constraints
- Availability of manpower, materials, etc.
- Your own intuition

Also seek answers to the following:

- Are all aspects of the solution sound and clear, and not complex?
- Will this solution achieve your objectives, i.e., will it solve the problem?
- What are the possibilities it will fail and in what way?

E. Planning action

Once you have found the solution, you are only 50% of the way there. A plan of action must be designed and successfully implemented if your solution is to have a chance to solve the problem at hand. Considerations in designing the plan of action are the following:

- Who is involved in the solution?
- Who will be affected by the solution?
- What course of action will be taken?
- How shall we present the course of action to company personnel, customers, vendors, etc.?
- How long will it take for the results to occur?
- Where will the solution take place?
- How will the solution unfold?
- What must occur for the solution to take place?

The plan of action should include a chart with projected dates detailing the steps necessary to arrive at the solution. Keep in mind that this is a projection and it's not written in stone. There might be a need to make modifictions in the time schedule because of unexpected events.

F.   Evaluating the plan of action

Once a solution has been chosen for implementation, it must be analyzed in regard to the following questions:

- Is the plan realistic, and feasible?
- Is there enough staff to carry out the plan?
- Is this plan comprehensive enough and yet easy enough? Will those affected know what is expected from them and how to carry it out?
- Will the plan embarrass anyone?
- Have any special conditions been overlooked?
- Who should be informed and involved?
- Who should be responsible for each aspect and/or phase?
- Is the plan of action cost effective?

To assure the successful implementation of your solution and plan of action, remember the following:

- Prepare and train your staff well in advance.
- If necessary hire new staff well in advance.
- Order necessary materials well in advance.
- Keep the communications line open. Use plenty of memos.

- Evaluate the effects of each phase as it is implemented and make whatever adjustments are necessary.
- Remain flexible and open-minded.

SUMMARY

The effectiveness of the first level sales management will play an integral part in the success of the salesforce. Assuming a company starts out with a solid strategic sales program, the first level sales manager will wear many hats as he leads his salesforce to achieve the criteria set forth. It is vitally important to have talented and capable personnel at this level, if top management is to gain the cooperation of the salesforce.

To ensure maximum results and reduced turnover, new personnel hired should be compatible with the management style of the person to whom they will be reporting. The working environment should also foster a positive feeling of cohesiveness among all employees to promote increased productivity.

One of the telling signs of the effectiveness of the sales manager is the ability to delegate authority and to supervise accordingly, because it is impossible to personally attend to all matters simultaneously. A good sales manager is the backbone of a good salesforce.

PART THREE

THE SELLING PROGRAM

III. GATHERING PROSPECTS

Probably one of the least favorite chores that salespersons
have to perform is cold canvassing. It can be the most demoralizing experience that anyone can go through. Some prospects will
let you go through your whole spiel and then say "no thank you",
others will flat-out reject you from the beginning. If the
prospect starts to engage in some dialog with the salesman, then
he stands a better chance of making the sale. Objections raised
by the prospect should not be viewed as obstacles but rather as
guidance provided as to what the prospect wants to be satisfactorily convinced of before he decides to buy your products. I am
not convinced that cold canvassing is the most efficient method of
finding new customers.

A quick method of identifying "hot prospects" should be the
theme of any prospecting program. An inquiry-generated method
followed up by the field salesforce can do away with a lot of wasted
and unproductive time. If the salesforce can increase the amount
of time spent on quality calls, this will translate itself in the
end into increased revenues. Salesmen should respond to inquiries
within 10 days of receipt, and quickly qualify the prospect either
for a follow-up field visit or for future mailings. Another

possibility is to further qualify them by telemarketing. More on this later. The salesman is an integral part of the success of this type of prospecting program. If he sits on the inquiry and follows up two months later, you can easily assess how "hot" that lead will be. The salesman must understand that this program is a supplement to his own efforts and certainly not meant as a put-down of his ability to find new customers. However, it is generally true that the acquisition of new customers is approached in a haphazard, intermittent, unplanned and uncoordinated fashion. Here are four general guidelines which are presented for your consideration in planning new customer acquisition.[8]

(1) SPECIFY: Decide what kind of customer is needed. This involves drawing up a customer "profile" using your present customers as a guideline. For instance you might decide that you are interested in customers within a specific region which can generate $100,000 per year in repeat purchases; or you might want independent distributors of products associated with the material handling industry in a major trading center in the southeastern region, having a salesforce of no less than five, carrying recognized domestic truck brands and calling on local industry, particularly food processors, etc.

(2) QUANTIFY: How many customers do you need this quarter of this
     year? Perhaps, to provide the type of business required, two
     new accounts with volume potential of $50,000 each are needed
     in each of the remaining quarters of the year, plus five new
     smaller accounts in each quarter with potential of $25,000 to
     $30,000 annually; or you may need an average of three new
     machine accounts each territory, each quarter, with the
     potential of supplying sales of $2,500 each year following
     installation. I caution you not to overlook the very real,
     often untapped, potential of existing accounts. By proper
     attention to maintenance selling, current accounts can be
     upgraded, expanded to new applications, and in effect become
     new for all practical purposes. If you neglect existing
     accounts, you are leaving the door open for competitors to
     take them away from you. In some cases it is far less costly
     to develop existing accounts than to acquire new ones.

(3) IDENTIFY: After you have specified and qualified the types
     and number of accounts wanted, the next step is to identify
     and rough screen the most likely candidates in the most direct
     and least expensive way. For a small local business the
     telephone directory can be used. A study of directories for
     several cities provides a fast, comprehensive, and specific

source of information for the significant trading center in a region. There are various sources that provide mailing lists using standard industrial classification (SIC) numbers, address, and names of relevant contacts. The purchase of one or more lists according to the developed specifications provides a fast way to be selective.

All things considered, given today's average cost of $100+ for an in-person industrial sales call, the time and money devoted to even modest pre-planning data research is well spent. This type of information can be found by using the following resources:

- U.S. Department of Commerce "Census of Manufactures" of "County Business Patterns".
- Dun & Brandstreet's various directories such as their Metal Working Directory, and Middle Market Directory.
- Various state industrial directories, trade association membership lists, local chamber of commerce and city directories.

(4) QUALIFY: One of the better sources of new accounts among existing users of a product or service is your direct or indirect competitor. Examination of the sales literature,

catalogs, and trade releases of a competitor often reveals a pattern of distribution, a listing of good reference ac- counts, and often the details of best applications. A frank discussion with some of your good customers will provide names of their competitors, who might become your customers as well.

Purchasing agents can be a most useful source of qualifying information because the agents talk to salesmen who talk to your competitors. In the field of selling, detailed attention to your competitor's activities can be equally as rewarding as attention to your customers, from the standpoint of identifying new customer opportunities, advantages, deficiencies, and needs. Do not over- look return of warranty or registration cards, which gives you information on the questions of the products users. Treat old customers the way you service new ones and you may not need so many new ones.

INQUIRY HANDLING

Typically, a great number of inquiries generated are a complete waste of time. Customers may not be sincerely interested in your product, or they might be curious to seeing what your offer is but do not have the authority to make the purchase. Consequently, an efficient method of prescreening inquiries is an important key in the reduction of wasted time and money. Let's review some of the methods used to increase effectiveness in utilizing sales inquiries:

1. By quickly answering inquiries within two days of receipt you are able to "strike while the iron is hot", and take advantage of your buyer interest while it is still there. Usually the request will be for additional information. Fulfillment packages should contain prices and technical information where applicable. The information should be presented in a clear and concise fashion so that anyone can understand your materials. Your information package can never be too simple.

2. To continue qualifying the prospect, get specific information on interests and intentions while, at the same time, gathering useful information for the marketing and sales department. Essentially about 8% of the initial group will respond a second time. This group can then be further qualified via telephone with a carefully prepared sales call or through additional sales literature. You will now be left with about 3% to 4% of your initial respondents. These names

and addresses can now be used to build a mailing list for
future mailings but, most important, they must be passed on
to the field personnel for prompt action.

Mailings to this list should be made several times a year to:

- Inform prospects of new company products, or new applications
- Continue to build interest by inviting more response
- Ask for more referrals, or ask if they wish to remain on the
  list

KEEPING TRACK OF COSTS

It is essential that a company have a firm grasp of all costs.
The cost of inquiries and their results is not an exception. By
simply dividing the inquiries received by the total cost of
obtaining them, you will come up with the cost per inquiry. After
a while you will determine which sources provide good leads and
which do not.   To determine the exact cost of new business,
accurate record-keeping is essential to calculate which leads were
converted into new business.   Salespersons must keep accurate
records of inquiry follow-up, and management must be involved if
the salesforce is to give the leads the swift attention necessary
to maximize opportunity.

An effective method of pre-screening is also important because management does not want to find itself in a position where they are dumping leads on the salesforce. If they do this, they will lose the sense of urgency among the salesforce and they can begin to be seen as a "nuisance", which in the final analysis will kill their effectiveness. The quality of leads handed to the salesforce must therefore always be of high caliber. I suggest providing a monthly computerized recap report, detailing inquiry follow-up, with copies distributed to the appropriate management personnel for their guidance. A high portion of lost sales in a given area can be a signal of potential problems; either the competition is beating you to the punch or you have a weak salesman.

More companies are turning to outside vendors to assist them in inquiry handling. Some of the more popular ones are:

- Qualified Lead System in New York, a unit of McGraw-Hill. They send fulfillment packages to prospects within 48 hours after receipt of inquiry; and within 10 days after the package is sent, a member of QLS will telephone the prospects with a carefully prepared text to determine the value of the lead.

- Lead Conversion System Industries, Clifton, NJ. They offer several options, providing toll-free "in wats" for client ads for direct mail. Their operators can direct callers to the nearest customer location, or further pre-qualify them.

I have provided the names of other companies who offer this type of service in Appendix A.

Once the salesforce is aware of quality of the leads that are presented to them, they will not look upon them as merely "coupon clippers" and not only will they provide the type of follow-up required but they may ask for more! If you provide mailings for your distributors and suddenly get a request for a large amount of pieces, chances are he is having some type of sales activity. Do not neglect to follow up and determine if you can provide additional support. This type of opportunity can assist you not only in building brand awareness but in providing information regarding potential problems.

QUALIFYING TRADE SHOW LEADS

Trade shows can provide an excellent source of sales leads for various reasons:

1.   The actual salesman who will sell the customer will qualify the prospect, consequently the salesman who will make later sales calls gets to meet the prospect in a "non-selling" environment and put the prospect at ease for the subsequent meetings.

2.   During the qualifying conversation, the salesman can usually gauge the intent of the prospect.

I suggest the prospect classification be determined as follows:

1. Has funds to buy and intent within three months
2. Has funds to buy and intent within six months
3. Has funds to buy and intent within one year

Convention results can be enhanced considerably by preparing the prospects prior to the event. Obtain the list of attendees if possible and mail press releases or a direct mail package. If the list cannot be obtained, do not overlook the possibility of renting a targeted list from one of the many list brokers. Also, advertising in trade publications would build customer awareness.

NETWORKING

Networking has become a popular method of building sales contacts with other sales executives calling on the same customers. One network asks its salespeople to bring names of three customers to each meeting, writing them on the back of their business cards and passing them out to the attendees. The rules are simple; make as many contacts as you can per meeting. This kind of networking can be an excellent source of leads. There is no pressure to "sell", the atmosphere is casual, and it's generally a fun way to pick up leads while socializing with your peers after hours to compare notes.

SUMMARY

A good sales prospecting program eliminates making useless sales calls on poorly defined prospects. By placing the salesforce in more face-to-face true selling situations, you are working with the law of averages. You are increasing the odds of selling more accounts because of the increased amount of opportunities.

Using such programs as direct mail, space advertising, tele-marketing, or trade shows can provide a body of pre-qualified prospects which can then be further classified into the degree of willingness to purchase. The leads determined to represent a real possibility of purchase within a three month period should be passed on to the salesforce for immediate follow-up. Other interested prospects should continue to be cultivated through periodic informative mailings, which provide the opportunity for the customer to let you know when he is ready to see a company representative.

IV. PRINCIPLES OF AN EFFECTIVE SELLING PROGRAM

Selling is not the act of calling on a prospect and reciting a memorized sales presentation with canned responses for answering objections. Productive selling is based upon offering the titi- lating features of your product or service, while simultaneously drawing the prospect into revealing what his needs are. Prospects turn into customers when they perceive that your widget will assist them in enhancing some part of their business and in turn bring them some type of reward, recognition, etc. The salesman can only begin to work towards accomplishing this once he has a clear understanding of the prospect's business and personal needs. This basic sales philosophy holds true whether calling on either a small firm or a large one. The ability of the salesperson to shape the prospect's perceptions concerning his product's features, cost and other pertinent factors will be reflected by the end result.

Calling on purchasing agents does not require any change in the basic sales philosophy. Purchasing agents do not suddenly become 100% objective or respond like emotionless robots. They also have the same desires and the same need to enhance their value to their employer.

THE EFFECTIVE SALESPERSON

An effective salesperson operates in much the same manner as an effective business. They both have a clear understanding of what it is they want to accomplish and a systemized approach to getting the job done. To start with the salesperson himself, I have witnessed too many instances of the "hire cheap" philosophy and it almost always results in high turnover. It's much too expensive in time and money to hire and train new personnel. I believe many executives are not fully aware of the full impact of this practice on the bottom line. When you start adding all the cost involved in interviewing, training, making up for costly mistakes and lost opportunities, it simply does not make economic sense to hire cheap.

When a sales territory becomes vacant an analysis is necessary of the type of customers being called on in this territory, to determine future potential and to assess the degree of skill required in the new salesperson to be hired. Do you in fact require another salesperson? Can you consolidate? Can you hire a service-type person to call on the large customers that require little if any "selling"? If you are not sure what type of person is called for, consider the following:

1. What education, experience, or factual knowledge or skills, will be required?

2. What training will be necessary?

3. What office activities will the salesperson be responsible for?

4. Will the salesperson perform duties such as sales planning, financial accounting, customer service, merchandising?

5. Will the salesperson be expected to solicit new customers?

6. What will be the specific selling duties, territory responsibilities, and call frequency?

The customer base (or territory) is the factor which determines the level of qualification required. One of the most frequently heard laments concerns the degree of difficulty in finding good salespeople. In part as I have said, this is caused by the mistake of searching for high-caliber personnel while offering low-caliber pay. You simply cannot afford to hire someone who is willing to settle for less money than he received from his last employer. A careful search below the apparent "reason" should be undertaken. Is this person really an order-taker who landed in a great opportunity before the employer discovered his mistake? Or is it a more serious matter?

CUSTOMER PLANNING

A critical prerequisite of effective selling is planning. The selling plan includes strategic information about present and prospective customers, and the plan of attack to achieve the sales forecast, divided by industry, geography if applicable, account classifications or any other workable unit. This systemized "cookie cutter" approach to the plan of attack can lead to a maximum selling effort. By essentially eliminating any guess work and providing direction, the selling plan enables the salesperson to maximize his opportunity to earn top bonuses and helps management to supervise and correctly evaluate its personnel.

The basic steps to be taken when setting sales strategy are the following:

- Develop a complete customer profile. This should include what your competitors are now selling the customer, and his established buying trends, i.e., are his requirements consistent all year or do they fluctuate? Be specific.
- Analyze the selling program of your competitors and profile their strengths and weakneses.

- Specify what you hope to gain, in dollars, unit sales, and number of new accounts.

- Determine how activity will be monitored, evaluated and by whom.

- When analyzing final results, look beyond the sales, especially if profit margins have decreased.

TRACKING COMPETITION

The days when a company would turn out a new product primarily because of its desire to utilize existing raw materials on idle machine time with little regard to the end-user is long gone. Product planning should evolve from customer needs. One strategy often used is to analyze carefully what your successful competitors are doing. What markets are they servicing? What are their product lines, prices, promotions, and methods of distribution? Dissecting the methods of your competition can provide you with greater insight into the reasons for their success and can give you guidance concerning methods of your own.

The flow of information from the field personnel to its headquarters is of vital importance in a successful selling program. Anyone who meets with customers is in a position to provide feedback which can be used by management in plotting the future direction of the company. Such people as product specialists, field engineers, service representatives, and sales representatives all spend time with the end-users, which can translate into vital feedback about customer needs and what the competition is offering. I must quickly remind you here that the act of trading information about consumers with your competitors through any form of direct contact is illegal.

Management should encourage its field personnel to report market activity to them, whether it's through an addition to the weekly reports or a quick inter-office memo. When the employee takes the time to write a memo reporting some activity, it would be appropriate to acknowledge the memo with some type of follow-up correspondence thanking him for his concern and/or report. If you don't respond, chances are the information flow will quickly dry up. This information should be passed along to the marketing department, which will in turn use the data if it is useful in planning long and short-term strategy.

It is important to gather and build a customer profile of both prospective and present customers. This should be updated systematically with new information obtained along with the purpose and results of each visit.

KEY ACCOUNT REPORTS: It's a good idea to set a criteria for what will constitute a key account. In the key account report, the salesperson should report activities, the purpose of his visits, tactics, and discussions with key account personnel. He should also suggest a future course of activities to increase revenue.

PROSPECTIVE ACCOUNT REPORTS: The prospective account report will provide management with an overview of the type of activity which has occurred in the pursuit of the account and, equally important, knowledge of what the competition is up to. In a chronological sequency, a history of activity should be kept, showing all interaction with this prospect.

If you are in a retailing business, it is advantageous to get repeat business. By building a data base of customers and utilizing computers to mail follow-up literature (such as mileage check-ups after so many miles, or clearance sales of fall fashions, etc.) you can build sales volume, retaining present customers through repeat business while continuing to attract new customers as well.

SELLING AS A SERVICE

The true act of selling is really not a selling act per se. It is a process of problem solving and with its conclusion comes the fulfillment of a customer need.

For example, a snack food salesperson offers to consolidate and arrange certain related but non-competitive items on his display if the customer agrees to sell his products. This solves the customer's problem of finding an attractive display, or, perhaps your company has the ability to provide a diversified range of products from one source, rather than dealing with many vendors, the customer can purchase all the products he needs from you. Another problem solved.

The question then becomes: When the salesperson calls on a customer, what exactly must he do to go about solving the problems which the customer himself may not be aware of?

1. Determine specific customer needs: The salesperson must find out all he can about the customer's business, and what kind of results he would want from your product or service. He must ask him what his needs are, because if he doesn't ask, chances are the customer won't tell him.

2. Select the product that can best fill the customer's needs:
   From past experience, the salesperson must carefully select
   the product that can best fill the needs of this customer. He
   should ask for help from others in the salesforce if necessary.

3. Demonstrate the product: Wherever possible, the salesforce
   should put your product to use, let the customer use the
   product, have him feel comfortable using it, and show him how
   it will meet his needs. You must prove value.

4. Follow-up: After the customer has agreed to buy from your
   company, the salesperson must not ignore him. This is
   probably the biggest complaint about salespeople. Usually it
   is caused in part by an overzealous salesperson promising the
   world while trying to land the account, and then only de-
   livering one small island. The sale is not completed until
   the customer's needs are fully satisfied.

The selling function is a series of analyses, recommendations, explanations, persuasions, and follow-ups. The affective
salesperson must study his marketplace carefully, be well prepared, and keep detailed and accurate records of all activities.

COLD CANVASSING

While I am generally opposed to cold canvassing because of its longshot possibilities of landing solid accounts, I do see a value in using it on an infrequent basis as a way of locating new firms starting up, or old ones expanding. Calling on strangers can also break the monotony of calling on the same people all the time and working in the same environment. What generally turns salespeople off about cold canvassing is the great numbers of rejections. After all, who likes to be consistently rejected?

PRODUCTIVE SELLING PROCESS

The selling process is comprised of different levels of difficulty. It is important to recognize the appropriate level of skill required to function at a given position. A firm is only as good as its salespeople. It would be highly inappropriate, for example, to place a good salesperson in a clerical position in the sales department. Sales positions can generally be classified into three categories:[9]

1. ORDER HANDLER. This is usually a knowledgable person with a good outgoing personality who deals with customers, sometimes processing customer payments.

2. ORDER TAKER. This can be the counter attendant at a fast food restaurant, or someone who orders merchandise to fill store shelves. Suggestion selling here can result in additional sales.

3. ORDER GETTER. This is the pure salesperson who makes sales presentations to new, and present customers. A great deal of sales inefficiency is caused by hiring too many order takers and placing them in order-getter positions.

CUSTOMER CONTACT

The salesperson must know something about the customers he calls on before he meets them. Acquiring the necessary knowledge will provide the ammunition to impress the recipient of his presentations. It will make the buyer take notice of the sales-person and provide him with the attention and interest required to make an effective sales presentation. This is one of the many important uses of a good updated customer profile.

PRODUCT KNOWLEDGE

There is nothing more offensive than a salesperson who wastes someone's time because of lack of product knowledge. Selling

is just like any other first meeting; first-impressions have a way
of staying with a customer for a long time. Make a negative first
impression and you will have a tough time turning it around. It
is the responsibility of management to encourage salespeople to
gain product knowledge through information made available to them
and through classes if necessary.

PRESENTATIONS

Here is where everything is brought together, the customer
profile, information gathered about his present and future needs,
and product knowledge. Put yourself in the prospect's shoes and
think about what you would want to know about your product or
service. Do not use a cookie-cutter approach to the actual sales
presentation. We live in an age of specialization, from foot
specialists to space consultants. Customize your presentation.
You have gathered all the pertinent data. Now it's time to
personalize it. Forget the canned presentation. I have yet to
meet someone who likes to speak to robots. Canned presentations
very rarely sound natural.

HANDLING OBJECTIONS

I used to be terrified of objections when I first started
selling. Then I realized that they represented progress towards
closing the sale! In other words, the customer is guiding you to
the knowledge of what will relieve his areas of doubt. Answer his
questions to his satisfaction and you will move closer to making
a sale. Again I must stress that you should not sound like a
recording. Personalize the answer as much as possible. Using such
techniques as counterquestions and restating objections will draw
the prospect into the presentation and in actuality assist you in
selling him.

SUGGESTION SELLING

Many salespeople are afraid to suggest other related items
when they have closed the sale for the fear of losing it. But the
best time to sell someone is after they have just bought from you.
The prospect offers less resistance and is usually very receptive
to the salesperson's suggestions.

FOLLOW-UP

The customer's relationship with your firm starts after the sale. In this day and age where competition is fierce, often there is little product differential between competitors. The sales person himself will often turn out to be the determining factor as to where a customer buys. Do not make promises which cannot be kept, be sincere, offer good and prompt service on customer request, and you will have a loyal customer for a long time.

Given the many roles a salesperson has to perform, what are some of the character traits which will enhance his chances of success?

- Judgment: Common sense, maturity and intelligence are interchangeable terms with judgment.
- Tact: Having a keen sense of what to say and when to say it, can eliminate many problems.
- Attitude: An employee with a good attitude will accept suggestions, learn, and apply creative selling processes. A bad attitude is contagious.

- Physical attributes: Personal appearance and personal hygiene are very important in the selling environment. Bad personal hygiene can lead to a bad first impression, which can be self-defeating.

PREPARATIONS

All industries have yearly cycles. You should investigate when business activity will be at its peak and its low point. During periods of relatively slow business activity, a salesperson can use the time to reflect on his client base and to get to know his customer and learn as much as possible about his business and its needs.

THE REVENUE STATEMENT

In the process of reviewing the customer base, a revenue statement per customer can be developed. This will indicate who your profitable customers are and generally indicate where your customers stand, whom to weed out, and with whom to alter your strategy. I again will stress the importance of not relying on dollar volume alone, although you will certainly require this information for your revenue statement. In the final analysis, unit sales will reveal what the real growth is.

In reviewing each customer history and emerging trends, you must be aware of customer needs and plan promotional activities such as off-peak season premiums or other services which will assist the customer in increasing his sales and in turn allow you to increase unit sales and revenue as well.

There are other steps which can be taken during any time of the year to cut down on expenses and increase efficiency. If you, or an employee of your firm, travel to a given town frequently and require lodging, arrange with a motel in town for a reduced rate in exchange for your company pledge of future business. Also in the course of visiting customers, it is a good possibility that you will develop friendships with other salesmen. Make arrangements with non-competitive sales personnel to plan your travel together and share the cost of hotels and automobiles.

BUYING COMMITTEES

Probably one of the toughest situations sales personnel can encounter is making a sales presentation to a committee. One may not know who the buying influentials are and consequently it is necessary to "work" all the committee members until one can determine where the power is located. Once the power has been

successfully located, the benefits of your product must be presented to the influential(s) so that they will represent a personal
gain for him and his company. Buying committees are formed for
various reasons; often to defuse a power struggle between individuals, or to get a consensus opinion on purchases of over $500,
thus insuring the need for such a purchase. They represent a
formidable task for the salesperson and therefore require especially strong preparation.

WHO IS THE BUYER?

The buyer in a buying committee can be recognized by the fact
that he will quickly become the focus of the meeting, whether he
speaks directly to the presenter or committee members seek his
feedback. A buyer is well informed about company operations, well
thought of by management, and can be on a "fast track". He
surrounds himself with good people, delegates responsibility, has
a high level of integrity, and has influence both in his firm and
in the industry.

What are some of the personal characteristics of a buyer? He
usually has strong concern for other people's perceptions about
him. This will influence his behavior and will manifest itself

in product selection. He often belongs to groups either defined or not; he does not want to stand out from the crowd,but to fit in. An up-and-coming person, he likes to emulate those who have made it; he is ambitious.

In contrast to buyers who are moving up, you have the leaders who have already made it. These fall into two categories: those who protect personal interest and are not interested in changing anything but in maintaining the status quo, and those who have a sense of social responsibility and do not want to damage the environment for the sake of making a buck. These people will go out of their way to remedy a wrong if they have the powers to do so. It is important to assess the type of person you are dealing with whenever possible.

REGIONAL SEGMENTATION

A great many firms in this day and age continue to treat their whole market as one. If your customer base is one of national scope, it would be more appropriate to listen to the needs of your customers on a regional basis and compare them to other regions. You might be bumping heads in one region with a long established firm which has developed a loyal following, and consequently you would have to change your appeal to offset the competitor's strength. Another possibility is that the market, because of its demographics, might be a totally different animal. For instance, car makers have long treated the west coast as a different market, in which the "standard" equipment includes many options for which others have to pay extra. The base sticker is higher to reflect the extra cost. The advertising is also different. Car makers in the west tend to emphasize technical details and often include a toll-free number to call for additional information. My point is that you must not randomly treat all customers alike because they are not.

PERSONNEL CHANGES

No matter how little turnover there is within your salesforce there is always a period of lost opportunities when such changes occur. The new salesperson must prove himself, establish his credibility and earn the trust of customers. However, this transition can be useful as a learning period when the outgoing salesman can ask the customer what he expects from him in the short-term and long-term. If the outgoing salesman has felt that he has not been able to please this customer, he should ask him why. This will not only help the new salesman but also alert the outgoing one as to a possible area he should be more cognizant of in the future.

It's also important to make sure to give the new salesperson's credentials, particularly if he has had similar sales experience within the industry. The larger the customer the more important the introduction becomes. After all, if a customer is giving your firm a substantial amount of business, he may have legitimate concerns about possible snags which may delay his orders and cost him money.

Today's environment places more importance on profitability than on sheer volume. Customers expect more from the products and good service from your company. There is very little tolerance for companies which cannot deliver products in a relatively short order cycle. Once you have captured a customer, you have only begun the actual selling program. It is your responsibility as management to make your company aware of what must be done to stay competitive in the market place. What type of service is expected from your service department? What kind of technology is needed? What kind of lead time is acceptable for re-orders, and/or new orders? Can computerization be integrated to coordinate and control your company's inventory movement? Your answers to these questions, along with your related suggestions, will not only enhance sales revenue, but will also make you a valued asset to your company.

COMPUTERS

If your company is one of the few which is not utilizing computers in its marketing and sales effort, it would be a gross understatement to say you are missing the boat. Let me provide you with two very brief examples of the application of computer to business needs.

By plugging a small personal computer into a telephone line, a real estate broker can show a prospective home owner what kinds of loans he can qualify for from a large pool of lenders, based on his income.

A retailer can use a personal computer to ask several questions about the customer's home furnishings. The computer then informs the customer where he will find whatever the store has to offer that can fulfill his needs.

To chose the best computer for your firm, list everything you would want it to do. Then visit several computer stores, ask to speak with a salesman and show him your list, carefully noting all he says. After a while you will have an idea who really knows what he's talking about and what type of equipment you should be looking at. The important point to remember is to select software (or programs) first and then the hardware (or the computer) that can run them.

SUMMARY

A successful selling program is one in which all the varied sales related components are meshed together to produce an efficient and productive effort. At the forefront of a good program is good sales personnel. By employing well-qualified personnel you are setting a solid foundation on which management can build to insure a solid future. The sales program must next build a good customer data base which will enhance the ability to prepare a workable strategic plan. This will enable the sales personnel to plan and prepare customized sales presentations to meet customer needs.

There must be good communication between field and staff personnel to keep the selling effort at its peak. Markets change because of different variables, which must be taken into consideration at the very least on a yearly basis. Management's inability to react to changing trends will eventually be reflected in increased costs and declining profitability.

V. IMAGINATIVE SALES APPROACHES

The sales profession can be very satisfying, but it can also cause one to fall into a rut. This can occur because of periods of little success or perhaps because of the lack of challenge felt in everyday activities. By constantly monitoring the market place, of both competitive and non-competitive companies, you can come up with new ideas which with some slight modifications can be adapted to your own selling effort. For instance, let's say you sell coffee, tea, and hot chocolate mixes. You would probably expect an increase of consumption during cold weather. If you keep an ear open to the weather forecast, you can increase advertising and promotions to coincide with upcoming cold weather and, as a result, increase sales during these periods.

Another concept currently being used in some parts of the country is one used by realtors. They send out low frequency radio signals over a one block radius to tell drivers about a particular house within that block in the hope of getting them out of the car to inspect the house. A sign in front of the home will tell passers-by where to tune in. Why not use this idea, if you are a retailer, to announce sales promotions and to attract customers into the store?

If you have a technical product, why not use audiovisuals to demonstrate your product in use? Sales presentation costs can be reduced by more than 50%, there is improved retention of message and the salesman is assisted in answering specific questions, which can lead to a sale. Check with any local audiovisual store and have them show you the array of equipment to choose from.

NON-TRADITIONAL SALES APPROACHES

The last few years have witnessed a rather large increase in sales seminars. The purpose of the seminar is to bring together your best prospects and, in a well-prepared presentation, give an overview of the state-of-the-art in your industry and how your company can provide them the benefits that make economic sense to them. Just from a "dollar and sense" point of view, think of how beneficial it is to have all your top prospects in the same room.

One way to make your seminar a success is to bring in outside speakers who are well-known in the industry and perhaps some present customers expressing why they are happy with your product. But don't expect the audience to sit through a whole day of speeches, no matter how interesting they might be. Utilize audiovisuals to bring your product to life under actual operating conditions.

SOME OTHER POINTS TO REMEMBER:

- Be thoroughly prepared, go through several dry runs to insure that everyone involved knows what to do and when to do it.

- Give all those who attend some back-up literature outlining your product benefits, and where to write or call if they want to inquire. Make it easy for them to act!

- Do not oversell! Don't keep your prospects to yourself; let them mingle with other prospects at the seminar. They will often discuss the materials heard, and your overselling may only alienate them.

- Be prepared to answer questions, study your product and the marketplace thoroughly.

Usually those who attend pay their own costs in getting to the seminar site and the sponsor (your company) will pay for expenses during the seminar. Don't forget to mail your prospects a meeting agenda upon their acceptance of your invitation. I cannot stress enough how an effective, well-planned and executed seminar can pay off towards your sales effort. After you have developed expertise in putting seminars together, you can prepare regional seminars throughout the country.

TRADE SHOWS

    While trade shows have been used successfully by many firms, I find some have been reluctant to try them because of a lack of knowledge of how to use this tool effectively. Even firms with experience in trade shows have hired trade show consultants to improve their effectiveness. Here are some tips to increase your trade show effectiveness:

- Selling in trade shows is no different from any other business endeavor. You must have a game plan going into it or you will accomplish exactly what you've put into it, nothing!

- Decide how much sales volume you want to attract as a direct result of trade show contacts in a specific period of time. Say you want to follow up on trade show leads and generate $300,000 worth of business within four months. The figure should at the very least cover the total cost of trade show participation.

- Set a goal of how many prospects each sales representative will see, per day, or whatever time frame is appropriate. Salespeople must set out with a basic set of goals and benchmarks which will tell them how they are progressing. Provide a clearly defined task which will assist in reaching the goal of securing the required number of leads per predetermined unit of measure.

Here are some helpful hints about how to qualify a prospect when screening trade show visitors:

1. What business is the prospect in?
2. Does he have the authority to purchase or can he influence the person who does purchase?
3. Does he have a genuine need for your product within the time frame set forth to close trade-generated leads?
4. Does this prospect represent a single company or a consortium? Does it buy your type of products? How frequently does it buy? What kind of financial condition is this company in? When are they likely to order?

This is the type of information which will qualify a prospect and provide you with maximum effectiveness in trade show participation.

INTERNATIONAL MARKETS

If your products can be sold overseas and you are not taking advantage of it, then you are not maximizing your product and profit potential. The quickest form of getting international representation is to find a commissioned sales agent. This can be done by contacting the prospective country's consulate in this country and simply asking them for assistance in locating an agent in their country. They may refer you elsewhere or if they have a publication, your company name can be included in their next issue. I know someone who received over 100 responses from one country from prospective agents using this method.

Once you have received enough names of prospective agents, it is preferable to visit the country firsthand. With the help of the consulates and other business development groups you may be referred to, go snooping around. Find out what the true market potential is. Who are your competitors? How are they selling your product? Once you have acquired some background information, you will then be in a good position to interview prospective agents. After a while you should be able to determine what type of candidate would best fit your needs.

Once you have found the agent you want to work with, clearly spell out your terms, conditions and commission structure. The laws in other countries can be vastly differnt from our own. Discuss the strategy which you want him to use in selling your product. In some countries lower prices are associated with inferior products. Also, do not try to translate your advertising into another language because it might not work. When General Motors tried to sell its Chevrolet Nova in some Latin countries, it found that the translation of Nova (no va) was "does not go!"

Expect to negotiate over such things as prices, mark-ups, commissions, etc. In many countries there are instances where better prices can be obtained compared to the going rate. Here are some helpful points to remember when looking for an international agent:

- Take your time locating a new agent. Use the proven techniques for finding one. Ask around. Talk to purchasing agents, other non-competitive agents, and get the opinions of others.

- If you currently have a capable agent, don't be too impatient. It's an expensive proposition to start over again.

- Make sure the agent is a native.

- Insure that the agent is trained well in your product line, and provide as much support as necessary to allow him to succeed.

- Make sure you check this person's reputation. Is he honest? Is he a loser? Ask around. After all, this person will become your company in this foreign country.

- What are his intentions concerning the amount of time and effort he will devote to your products? Extensive travel and use of additional personnel will give your product the kind of exposure it must have to enhance its chances of success.

MOTIVATION AND INCENTIVES

It can safely be assumed that salespeople are motivated by money! Many firms have gone beyond the traditional methods of allowing salesmen the opportunity of making extra money, providing new methods of motivation in an effort to increase sales revenues.

CONTESTS   One firm I know kept trace of display footage obtained on new customers compiled during a specified contest period. Salesmen were then given a catalog of gifts they could select. Each gift "cost" so many feet. The gifts included television sets, stereos, and other quality items.

Other awards can range from trips to Hawaii to gold coins. However, do not expect miracles when the rewards are meager.

TIME OFF   Compensating sales people with extra days off, such as Fridays, to allow for a longer weekend will allow them to spend more time with their families as well as time to get away from the daily grind.

TRAINING   Providing either more in-house workshop course or outside seminars will give sales personnel a different
perspective on their job functions. A good seminar will
make you re-evaluate your approach to conducting your
business and perhaps cause you to make small alterations
which can result in increased efficiency. Even if no
change occurs, I believe the mere act of re-evaluating
what you do, with a different set of criteria, is
beneficial.

INCENTIVES   No matter how well a marketing strategy has been
carefully thought out and planned, absolutely nothing
will happen if the salespeople do not go out and make it
happen. Selling is a highly emotional activity. If the
salesperson is not excited about selling his product, it
will be reflected in the final results. This is, in
part, why sales incentives will always remain a popular
format for getting an extra effort from the salesforce.
If a straight bonus over base quota is to be used, a
basic 80% of quota should be met before qualifying for
any additional bonuses.

Such rewards as gifts, issues of company stock, or any other non-monitary reward will serve as a constant reminder of a job well done. An increasingly popular gift is a personal computer, which will also benefit the company from the salesperson's increased productivity.

Here are some helpful ideas for running an effective incentive program:

- Before deciding what the rewards will be, get feedback from the sales staff. They are the ones you want to motivate. Discuss with them not only what would interest them but also the quotas to be set to qualify for these rewards.
- Do not copy what your competitors are doing! Try to be original and if possible make your incentive program more attractive than your competitor's program.
- Come up with a contest theme that will appear on all correspondence during the contest period. This will accomplish two things: it will maintain enthusiasm within the salesforce, and re-enforce the company's good intentions towards the salesforce.

- Do not judge trainees by the same criteria as experienced personnel. Set up different methods of evaluation, such as number of calls made, account upgrading, etc. You simply cannot expect the same results from a trainee that you would from an experienced sales representative.

- Send weekly updates to the salesperson's home regarding incentive-related activity. He will probably be more likely to read it at home and possibly the family may become aware of it and provide a little more incentive to perform.

- Make the chances of winning some type of reward possible for at least one third of the salesforce.

- Do not become predictable and schedule incentives at the same periods every year if at all possible. However, a good time to become predictable if you must, with minimal loss of effectiveness, is during new selling seasons or any other period where the salesforce cannot hold back before the incentive dates.

- Try to conduct incentive periods after new skills are learned, such as after an in-house workshop/seminar. Used in this fashion the incentive period will have a two-pronged effect: it will re-enforce a new sales skill and lead to a continuous program of sales motivation.

SALES AWARDS

Sales awards are used to achieve and surpass sales forecasts, and to provide a permanent reminder of outstanding sales performance. Some companies are now using super bowl type rings to reward sales excellence over a period of years, or special blazers. In some cases the chief officer will send a note praising the salesperson's efforts. Regardless of the method used, the important point to remember is to build a program that motivates as many people as possible.

SPECIAL EVENTS

Special events are another popular and effective method of motivating the troops. Probably the most celebrated of all companies to put on the ultimate special event is Mary Kay Cosmetics. The firm annually spends millions in addition to $1 million dollars given away in diamonds and furs -- even the husbands get diamond rings. Some companies will have an award banquet as a yearly event, which features such things as hanging larger-than-life pictures of the winners.

MEASURING SALES PERFORMANCE

After all is said and done by the salesforce, there comes a time at least once per year when an evaluation of performance must be filled out. This serves essentially two purposes:

1. To determine the performance level attained since the last evaluation
2. To point out areas where the salesperson needs to improve

Based on these two factors and on company profitability, a determination will be made about the future this person can look forward to. Immediate decisions such as amount of salary increase, promotion, demotion or termination are made by using performance appraisals.

Some of the criteria used for measuring performance should include the following:[10]

1. Sales Volume. If you are comparing one year to the next, do not neglect to break it down into units, especially if there have been price increase.

2. Amount of time spent in the office. Did this person spend a lot of unnecessary time in the office when he could have been more productive out in the field?

3. Personal appearance. Does this person project the type of image which top management would approve? In some areas it's perfectly acceptable to dress without a tie, but in other areas it's totally unacceptable.

4. Number of sales calls made on existing accounts. Perhaps involvement in a special project seriously curtailed his ability to make the required number of calls. Do not judge results on face value; look beyond as well.

5. Number of new accounts. Management must have an idea as to the potential new business available to be able to judge accurately the salesperson's output.

6. Completeness and accuracy of sales orders. Does the home office have to return orders submitted by the salesperson to complete the paper work? Is it sloppy? Is it accurate?

7. Promptness in submitting reports. Does the salesperson submit reports on a timely basis or are they always late, causing customers to complain?

8. Dollars spent entertaining customers. Is this salesperson using discretion in entertaining? Did he spend $300.00 a year on a customer who purchased $100.00 worth of products for the year with no potential for further sales growth?

9. Does the salesperson sell the company? Does he "talk up" the company name to his customers, a practice which leads to customer referrals or purchases from another division, etc.

10. Accuracy in quoting prices and deliveries. There is nothing more self-defeating than calling a customer to tell him that you made an error in your price quotation after he has accepted it; or misquoting actual delivery dates and causing possible scheduling problems for the customer.

11. Knowledge of the business. Does the salesperson know his business well enough for the amount of time he has been working in it? A lack of knowledge might be a tip-off of a lack of interest in either the job or the company.

12. Planning the work schedule. Is there too much time lost because of a lack of planning?

It would be appropriate after going over the performance appraisal to develop a personalized guide in which the salesperson is given specific guidelines for improving sales performance. A copy of this form should be given to him to keep and to refer to during the course of the year. Here is a suggested format to be used in preparing a guide for improving performance:

A. <u>Planning</u>

Get the sales representative's agreement about goals to attain or exceed for the upcoming year.

Designate the profit contribution in dollars (and units) for each major product line, each major market, and target accounts.

Plan the representative's expenses for the upcoming year, and make a commitment for the following:

- The total expense budget in dollars
- Dollars to be allocated for travel, entertainment, telephone and other expenses

B. <u>Measuring</u>

Review, at least monthly, the representative's record for:

1. Year-to-date progress toward 12-month profit contribution goals
2. Year-to-date budget compliance

C. <u>Correcting</u>

Meet with the sales representative if his record is 10% or more off target. Review the number of calls made on each significant account along with what he feels are his problems and accomplishments. In addition, you may need to do some of the following to help improve performance:

- Give more day-to-day help and direction
- Accompany on calls to provide coaching
- Conduct regular meetings on subjects that the representative wants covered
- Increase sales promotion activities
- Transfer accounts to other sales representatives if there is insufficient effort or progress
- Set tighter control over price variances allowed
- Increase or reduce selling price
- Add new products or services
- Increase financial incentives
- Transfer, replace, or discharge the representative

If a thorough job is done in both the performance appraisal and the guide for improving performance, there should be absolutely no room for doubt as to what is expected from the sales representative. If he understands what is expected of him, you are in fact assisting him to succeed; and by helping him, you as the manager are helping yourself as well.

THE EMOTIONAL FACTOR

I have been around selling long enough to recognize that without positive emotions nothing outstanding can occur. A strong desire to sell can almost always produce greater results than a lot of ability without real desire. I can give you an example of the emotional factor at work in one specific instance. When I was a District Sales Manager for a well-known national snack food company, I had one territory which was a thorn in my side. It was situated in a rather undesirable area, which coincidentally was the lowest producing territory in the region. The salesmen were compensated on a base salary and weekly commission after a pre-determined volume was reached. As a result this territory had a revolving door as salesmen requested to be transferred out just as soon as they got in. Finally I was given a substitute salesman to fill in while we contemplated dividing this troubled territory among the existing surrounding territories to absorb all the accounts.

What we thought of as just a substitute salesman turned out to be a heavyweight champ. He was hired to help us out during periods of increased selling activities in the hope that he could help pick up some of the slack. Within the first couple of weeks

I noticed a marked increase in the volume generated by our "helper". I started spending more time with him out in the field, and insuring that he had an ample supply of display equipment as he had requested. The most noticeable trait about this man was the enthusiasm he generated when he spoke to prospective customers as well as present customers. He was excited about his product; he believed in what he was saying, and the prospect could not help but give this product a chance. It also did not hurt that, at about the same time, the firm was starting to advertise heavily; but, then again, many others had the opportunity to take advantage of the same variable and neglected to do so. Let me end this story by reporting that in a year-and-a-half, this territory went from ranking dead last out of a total of 40 plus territories in the region to the "top" of the heap with a healthy weekly paycheck for the salesperson to match.

Could all the salesmen in this firm have attained the same dramatic results? Probably they could not have developed the same type of volume increase, but certainly, in my opinion each territory had a lot more room for growth. My assigned district accomplished the following:

- Increased district sales by more than 40%
- Achieved territory sales averages that were at least 15% higher than the next closest district
- Realized close to 120% of sales forecast, at a time when most districts were averaging near 90%
- Total new accounts in one year exceeded more than 65% increase (About one third of the new accounts were obtained by you know who).

During my stint as District Sales Manager, I was able to get a lot of mileage from my salesforce and was constantly asked what my "secret" was? I always gave the same response, "Listen to your salespeople, treat them as you would want to be treated, and provide the support they require to perform." Apparently they were not convinced it could be so easy because they would also ask my colleagues "How does he do it?"

I was not then, or now, a perpetual cheerleader because I find this type of mentality most annoying. When I sat down with each salesman to discuss sales projections for the following quarter or year, I depended on their input heavily. In a few weeks we would sit down again and further refine our expectations, adjusting them either up or down. I found that the salesmen would consistently

give me a pretty fair assessment of their territory's potential.
Except for one older salesman I had, who was old enough to be my
father. I discovered that if I cut his territory (he was compensated for the lost revenue for a period of two-and-a-half
months) he would quickly match the same sales volume prior to my
alterations. Consequently, we played this game for a few years
with always the same predictable results until he retired.

Many firms treat their salespeople as second or third-rate
citizens. Selling as I have stated before, is a highly emotional
act. The average salesperson has three rejections to every one
success; consequently, if he receives similar negative vibes at
his workplace, there is no question in my mind it will eventually
affect his output. This is one of the most common phenomenons I
have witnessed repeatedly. Management makes more and more demands
on the salesforce, while using a whip and chain to motivate them!
Then management will say something like "We have to hire some good
sales talent if we are going to hit our five year projections."
Management must set the tone to create the environment which will
make the salesman feel as though he is part of the company and not
an outsider.

SUMMARY

Management must always be on the lookout for new and inno-
vative sales approaches which can provide the firm with a competitive advantage. By paying close attention to both competitive
and non-competitive companies, it can learn of different selling
approaches which in some instances can be adapted for their own use
with small alterations, if any. Management must consistently
re-evaluate its marketing and sales program to look for methods
where it can trim away the fat and/or increase efficiency.

Do not overlook the use of seminars, trade shows, and the
international market as methods of expanding distribution of your
product. Sales presentations themselves can be upgraded by using
such techniques as low frequency radio signals, and the whole array
of audiovisuals to re-enforce the sales message.

Keeping the morale of the salesforce high must be an objective
in any successful selling program. The use of incentives such as
monetary rewards, quality gifts, momentoes, or trips can play an
important role in sustaining high morale.

Yearly evaluation should accomplish two things; a determination of the performance level attained since the last evaluation, and the identification of specific areas where improvement
is expected. Clearly identifying both positive and negative areas
of performance, will also guide first level management into the
areas where a concentrated effort should be instituted. Subse-
quently, the salesman should understand where he stands and how
well he is contributing to the overall selling effort.

V. MEETINGS

If you do not currently schedule and hold regular meetings with your salesforce, it's time to start. The frequency of these meetings will depend on the availability of your sales personnel. I think it's a good idea to include the support staff in these meetings as well because they are the administrative extension of the salesforce. They should be kept abreast of what the sales-force is trying to accomplish so that they can appreciate the urgency and/or consequences involved in a given sales opportunity.

My first sales job was with an industrial firm which held sales meetings every Monday morning to discuss upcoming weekly activities. Problems and growing trends were thrown out for group discussion, and any variables which affected their business were noted. This particular department only had about ten sales people but we often had a plant manager in on the meetings when he was in town, and other support personnel were there whenever possible. These meetings not only served as an ongoing education in sales but made everyone a more complete salesman because of the wealth of knowledge we had about our company and the industry. In fact salesmen from this firm usually were presented with plenty of employment opportunities within the industry because of their knowledge of the industry.

Regional or national sales meetings should be held every year. Management objectives in preparing the agenda should be: to increase the salesman's awareness of his job, responsibilities, and importance to his company; to increase his product knoweldge and its applications to the applicable markets; and finally to encourage increased communication and cooperation between field personnel and headquarters.

Sales meetings can easily become a one way affair where the salesforce merely yesses you to death, and quickly returns to old habits once back in their territories. You must make the meeting basically one which fosters learning through participation. For example, attendees can be divided into various smaller groups where seminar/workshops can be held on different subject matter. At the end of an hour, the groups should be switched to a different seminar/workshop until everyone has attended each one. By working this way, you encourage participation, which is the best way to learn. You also accomplish far more than you can with a much larger group. Not too many people like to raise their hands and raise questions -- let alone carry on a conversation -- in front of a large group.

However, there will be portions of the meeting where it just makes more sense to have one large presentation -- the president's message, for example. The first bit of advice I can offer is to rehearse, and rehearse again, especially if you are including audiovisuals in the presentation, which I strongly suggest. There is nothing more embarrassing and unprofessional than a presentation which is out of synch with its pictures. It would be the equivalent of reading a magazine with the captions placed under the wrong pictures. Audiovisuals play an important role in maintaining audience interest while you deliver your message. I have listened to many speakers, some very prominent in their field, who bored their audience to death. Why? Because they prepared a fine speech but proceeded to stand up before the audience without any audiovisuals and either read their notes or recite a memorized speech. Boring! I am not saying that you must attain the skills of an actor, but learn how to break up your presentation to ensure maximum audience reception.

When preparing the agenda, try to carefully balance the speakers so that you do not end up with three boring speakers in a row! Carefully edit all speeches to ensure continuity of the meeting's theme and general interest. Get some of your sales people involved. If one person is particularly strong in one area, have him share his methods with his peers. Allow plenty of time at the end of the presentation for questions and answers. If the meeting is held in a resort area, start and finish early to allow time for recreation.

When planning meetings in resort areas, plenty of time should be allowed to personally check the site and finalize all arrangements such as special equipment needs. The company should pick up travel, food, and hotel expenses. All meetings should be completed in three days. After that point the attendees become restless and not much is accomplished. Be careful not to accept those "special" meeting rates that seem too good to pass up. Having a meeting in a beautiful Florida location in July will make you many enemies.

While national sales meetings are popular, they are expensive! A growing number of firms prefer the regional type of gathering. Instead of a national meeting, several regional meetings of the one-day variety can be arranged at an airport hotel, centrally located in the region. Sales personnel can fly in early in the morning and leave in the evening, paying only for their travel and lunch.

Some other steps taken to cut the cost of meetings include: cutting the length of the meetings, eliminating the frills, avoiding the "famous" meeting places, using one of your own facilities, scheduling the meeting to allow the attendees to take advantage of special fare reduction programs offered by the airlines and, finally, combining the meeting with another event such as the end of a convention.

TELECONFERENCING

Another alternative to bringing people to one location is the teleconference route. This is an excellent method for presenting your message simultaneously to a large number of people at different locations. Conference sites are chosen -- usually a hotel -- where the hotel assumes the responsibility for arranging the satellite transmission, receiving services, and large screen(s) at the meeting room. Although the cost of the event can run as high as $100,000 per hour, it may in many instances turn out to be far cheaper than flying personnel in. Once you start to tally up transportation costs, lodging, food, and salaries it can become a costly proposition. But through teleconferencing you can reach far more people, while your costs do not increase as much proportionally as compared to a live visit to the meeting sight.

In planning the teleconference, careful thought should be given to what is to be presented. Time is money. To keep your teleconference moving you must balance humor, the proper combination of executives, and a good variety of camera angles. Probably the most popular use of teleconferencing has been to introduce new products. Here are some tips to assist you in planning a teleconference:

- Plan carefully what you want to say and how much information you want to present. Don't overwhelm your audience. Take advantage of the special effects available such as videotaped inserts, computer graphics, and edit - ing to keep your presentation moving.

- Review all speeches and edit for content, general interest, and brevity.

- Make sure to rehearse the teleconference on the "set", and include all props, cueing and any other effects which will be used. By doing this, everyone will have a chance to present his portion and get his feet wet. The entire program can be evaluated, necessary changes can be made, and the whole presentation can be timed. Always prepare additional materials in case you have time left over. It's better to be ready with additional material than to try to bluff your way along.

SUMMARY

Sales meetings should be a regular part of your sales program. They are an effective method of assisting sales personnel in performing their job through group discussion of market conditions and other variables which have an effect on their ability to perform. The sales manager can use his knowledge and the experience of other personnel to assist the salesmen to become more efficient contributors. More frequent meetings are always "preferred"; however, if the salesmen are spread out geographically fewer regional meetings should be held. It is always a good idea to have a national sales meeting -- either in person or through teleconferencing -- whenever possible to foster camaraderie, increase job skills, and enhance sales performance.

PART FOUR

SPECIALIZED SALES PROGRAMS

VII. INDEPENDENT AGENTS

As I have pointed out, it does not make economic sense to maintain company sales people in unproductive areas. Low volume territories are ideally suited for independent sales agents, also referred to as manufacturer's agents, or manufacturer's representatives. Here are some guidelines for determining what factors would make a product suitable to be sold through independent agents:

1. The product should have a good selling potential in the agent's given area.
2. The product should be a standard non-customized item.
3. The product should be capable of being sold in small quantities.
4. The product should be an item that requires quick availability, and a low level of supervisory approval for purchase.

It may be feasible to have more than one agent handling different products in your product line in the same area, either because they call on different industries or different end-users. On the other hand when products require a special personal touch or service, the company may need to control the entire selling job.

A. TERRITORIES[11]

What is your goal for each specific territory? If you had the best salesforce money could buy, could your goal be achieved? If you could get only mediocre employees, what maximum dollar volume would you set for their quota? What is your present dollar volume in the territory? What does it cost to bring in that volume? Based on the cost figures, what would your cost of sales be for achieving your ultimate sales quota? How many dollars do you have to invest to build up a specific territory? Does the investment run over a long period of time, which will allow a mediocre sales staff to reach its objective?

B. SELLING

What type of salesperson do you need: an order handler, order taker, or order getter? Does the selling process demand technical or non-technical knowledge to "sell" the product effectively? What are the selling practices in your industry? All these issues should be identified and policy set forward when looking for, and working with, an independent agent.

C. MARKET PENETRATION

How well do you know this market? Are you asking the agent to penetrate? Can you offer guidance or will you rely on his knowledge for his given area? What is the required frequency of sales calls? Does he have enough manpower to handle the task at hand? How quickly do you want to penetrate this market? Does this agent have the potential to accomplish it?

D. COST

While you are not paying someone to call directly on customers in this area, expect to pay commission on sales to the agent. You will have to pay the clerical staff to take care of agent requests and to process paperwork generated by the agents. Let's evaluate the merits of securing the service of independent agents.

TRAINING - Independent agents can be put in the field quickly, and the training cost is nominal.

TYPES OF SELLING - Agents are specialists, seldom offer service selling, have an established customer base, and sell in a given territory with a specific product.

EXPERIENCE - Most agents are experienced professionals.

SELLING TIME - An agent devotes only part time to your products. If your product has little demand there is a danger of even less selling effort.

OPENING NEW TERRITORIES - Established agents offer a built-in following in given territories and have in-depth knowledge of their territories.

COST - An agent gets paid only when he sells your product. All expenses incurred by him are on his account.

PAPERWORK - Only commission statements need to be issued.

CONTROL - The agent is free to operate according to the prior agreed-upon terms and conditions.

Some of the advantages of using a sales agent are:

- Quick territory entry
- Regular calls on customers and prospects
- Quality experienced salesmanship at low cost

Some of the disadvantages are:

- You have limited control over their selling techniques.
- On large volume sales the selling expense may be excessive, greater than it would be with your own employees.
- You do not have total allegiance because of the wide array of companies he may represent.
- Upon termination of your agreement with an agent, you may lose many customers.

SELECTING AN AGENT

If you have never had any experience in finding and choosing agents, where do you go? First stop would be to read trade publictions whose readership is geared toward the type of manufacturer's representative you are seeking. Recommendations from customers and sales managers of non-competing companies in your industry are also helpful. Also editors or salesmen from trade magazines can offer recommendations.

Once you have located some potential agents, keep these points in mind. Do not choose agents who are already overloaded with other products, and avoid small or under-financed prospective agents. Keep in mind that the more successful agent will probably have other firms pursuing him for representation. If your products are of a technical nature which would require assistance, then it would be best to choose an agent with a small product line. If you spot a small-sized potential agent with some promise, do not be afraid to consider helping finance or support him in the hope of building a future profitable association. This might entail having the agent spend time with your organization as well as travelling with your salesman. If the market you wish to penetrate is too large for one agent's organization, do not hesitate to commission other agents. However, do not saturate a market, because then it will not become a profitable item for a given agent and you risk the chance of losing the agent's full support.

By the same token do not hesitate to terminate your agent's working agreement if you feel he is not aggressive enough either because of lack of interest or because he has added new product lines. It does not hurt to always be on the lookout for prospective agents with more financial firepower, selling muscle, or whatever your needs are.

The following are some guidelines for consideration when selecting an agent(s) organization:

1. Agents should be calling on the same market that interests you, with related products (although not competitive).

2. The agent's territory should be a good match with the trading areas you want covered, and not generally overlap with another agent's areas.

3. The agent's selling style should agree with your company's basic philosophy. For example you do not want a high-pressure agent selling your products if your policy is against that approach with company-hired salesmen.

4. The lag time of commission payments should be similar to the agent's other product lines. And the financial conditions should generally indicate his ability to sustain your commission cycle.

5. The size of the agent organization should be one that will allow coverage of the geographic agreed-upon market, and one that will have aggressive sales representatives and minimum turnover.

WORKING WITH AN AGENT

A written contract or agreement is the proper method to start harmonious relations with an agent. The agreement should clearly list all that is expected from both parties. You cannot hire an agent, provide some materials, and sit back and expect the sales to start rolling in! It is also necessary to work with and motivate the agent. Some of the steps to be taken can include:

- Having meetings to discuss competitive trends and future strategy, while at the same time assisting agent operations.
- Listening closely to their suggestions as to what your company should do to enhance the marketability of your products.
- Keeping them well-informed of your company's activities, especially those that would affect them. Newsletters are an excellent tool for this purpose.
- Placing toll-free numbers on ads and redirecting leads to the appropriate agent.
- Setting up an escalating commission structure with either new agents or with established ones on a yearly basis.
- Providing some type of co-op advertising allowance to promote your products.

We have looked at some of the reasons a product would be suitable for independent agent representation. There are also organizational reasons that would suggest that agent representation would make a great deal of sense. They are as follows:

1. The company simply cannot afford to hire direct sales personnel.

2. Because of normal or high turnover, there is a need for long-term continuity between sales representatives and customers.

3. Entering a new market is of major importance.

4. The market is too small or marginal to support a direct salesman.

5. You are currently dealing with other agents and find it profitable.

Once you have established an agent network, once a year an evaluation should be reviewed by the appropriate members of management. Strategic action plans should be formulated to determine what is to be accomplished in the upcoming year, which may or may not include finding a new agent. Some of the essential points for agent review should include:

1. Level of experience indicated through the quality of service rendered

2. Coverage of area agreed-upon, and time devoted to seeking new business

3. Management capabilities as demonstrated by results of inventory control, warehousing, record keeping, sales management, and financial management.

4. Actual sales volume compared to company performance standard, and market share.

5. Willingness to co-operate with company policies and guidelines

6. Potential and capabilities for growth in the assigned area

SELLING PRODUCTS ON CONSIGNMENT[12]

Selling on consignment can be used as a marketing tool which creates no obligation on the part of the dealer in the event the product does not sell. This arrangement can be attractive for both the wholesaler as well as the retail dealer to stock your product at no risk to him. Here are some of the advantages of consignment selling:

1. It allows the seller to increase the exposure to the buying market.

2. It provides incentive to the wholesaler and/or retailer to try out the item at no cost to him.

3. It increases the opportunity for newly-introduced or seasonal merchandise to be stocked despite lack of demand.

4. It provides the manufacturer with the opportunity to have the merchandise exposed to the buying public instead of having it die a slow death in some isolated warehouse.
5. It can be used for market testing: off-price, size of packaging, etc.

In deciding whether or not to use consignment in selling your product, consider these disadvantages:

1. While the merchandise is being exposed, you get no money until the sale.
2. As a manufacturer you must have enough cash on hand for extended periods until the merchandise is paid for.
3. Merchandise is subject to shopper abuse, damage and theft.
4. You cannot control shelving decisions since consignees have no capital invested in your inventory and may favor outright--owned inventory and promoting as well.
5. If the gross margin to the seller is greater than the percentage commission with the sales of consigned goods, then the seller may tend to favor selling outright-owned goods.

Keep in mind that the consignee never takes title to the merchandise but acts as the agent of the consignor to pass title to the buyer. Since title does not pass to the consignee in the absence of an agreement, liability for loss of the merchandise remains with the consignor. The consignee can agree to specific statements for assuming a share of the loss in case of shoplifting or other damage to the merchandise. However, in the absence of such an agreement, you the consignor, are responsible for the loss involved even though the merchandise might have been shoplifted from the premises of the seller while the consignee exercised normal care in the display and handling of the merchandise.

When placing the merchandise with the wholesaler or retailer, you might agree in writing to place merchandise where it will be exposed to an estimated 50% of foot traffic. Also agree upon the exact commission to be paid upon the sale of the merchandise, length of time to keep merchandise, and the intervals in which the consignee will make payments on goods sold. Do not forget agreements concerning delivery and pick up of merchandise, and conditions or storage of any merchandise that is not being displayed.

Agreements are particularly necessary for perishable merchandise. Make it understood that damaged goods are to be returned to you; otherwise the consignee can claim to have disposed of these when he might in fact have sold them and kept the money. You may be able to find a consignee who will assume part or all losses for damaged goods.

CONSIGNOR'S LIABILITY

Whenever merchandise is destroyed by water, fire or smoke while in the inventory of the consignee, the loss is that of the consignor. The importance of this issue calls for special attention at this point because there is a sales situation which has been viewed by some as similar to consignment selling and can become a legal problem for the consignor. "Sale or return", as it is called, is a situation in which the risk of loss passes to the consignee when the goods are in his possession. Certain points have surfaced that are important in the determination of "true consignment" according to the courts:

1. The consignor is authorized to demand return of the goods at any time.
2. The title rests with the consignor until the goods are sold, at which point, title moves directly to the buyer and never passes through the consignee.
3. The consignee is authorized to sell the goods only at a specified price or not less than the invoice amount.

4. The consignee is required to meet certain standards in keeping of the goods, such as their segretation from goods wholly-owned or held under a claim of ownership or interest.

5. The consignee is required to forward proceeds of sale immediately to the consignor or to deposit them in a special account.

If you plan to sell on consignment, your attorney can provide guidance on the legal aspects, and your accountant can advise on the record keeping and accounting aspects of this type of selling.

SUMMARY

The use of independent sales agents can be successfully integrated into any selling program. Whether used exclusively or in conjunction with company salesmen to cover isolated territories, agents can offer the ready-made customer base of his existing customers plus valuable insight into his selling region.

Considerable care must be taken when selecting an independent agent to represent your firm. After one is chosen, duties, responsibilities and financial arrangement should be clearly spelled out to avoid future misunderstandings. Have the agent spend time at your location as well as with other salesmen to acquaint himself with all the facets of your selling program.

VIII. TELEMARKETING

The role of the telephone in the selling process continues to increase in importance as the cost of selling escalates. There are many uses such as direct sales, locating dealers, providing customer service, canvassing, certifying orders, advertising messages, and gathering credit information, to name just a few.

It can provide an effective and economical method of reaching prospective buyers and determining customer appeal, new product uses and applications, or problems you were not aware of. There are two types of in-house phone programs:

INBOUND TELEPHONE - This is where calls are generally received on an 800 number. These calls can be taken by scripted operators working from either a computer screen or a typed script.

OUTBOUND TELEPHONE - This program requires operators with sales-oriented personalities and the ability to close a sale. Consequently, you need personnel who are good communicators and experienced sales supervisors.

Unless your operation is one where there is a constant flow of telephone activity, it does not pay to maintain an in-house telephone center. Anything less than capable and experienced personnel can cause more harm than good. Inquiries must be handled immediately, or prospects will get a negative view of the company. Also, hot leads have a way of becoming cold if not acted upon promptly.

If you do decide to set up your own in-house telephone center, here are some of the elements you should take into consideration:

PERSONNEL - The hiring and training of the staff is of the utmost importance. It would be a good idea to hire an experienced telemarketing professional as either a manager or consultant.

EQUIPMENT - Again, someone with prior experience can provide insight as to the requirements for the type of program you desire. Past research has indicated that the use of light-weight headsets for telemarketing has increased the rate of employee effectiveness.

PROSPECT LISTS - This list can be made up of either your own company's past or current customers, or one that has been carefully chosen from a list broker using existing customers as a profile. When calculating costs make sure to include the expenditures involved in cleansing the list periodically to keep the list fresh.

COORDINATING THE EFFORT - It is a foregone conclusion that the combination of the direct mail effort with telemarketing follow-up will produce anywhere from 2 to 7 times greater response.

Once you have determined the scope of your telemarketing effort it is time to decide exactly what you want it to accomplish. Is it going to be used for market research, advertising, direct mail follow-up, or as an extension of the selling effort? During the planning stages, identify the different market segments which you want to sell to and strategies to be used in each segment. Within each market divide prospects into large, medium, and small. The approach for each segment should vary since their needs will vary. In setting objectives provisions must be made for measuring results, using such factors as the number of calls per day, the cost of calls, the sales versus cost ratio, and the time period involved. Detail specifically what must be done, and be prepared to take appropriate action if you do not get the desired results.

Here are four major areas of concern in plotting out the campaign:

1. Market segment: As in direct marketing, the customer list is the most important element of the telemarketing effort. The best prospects are those who are familiar with your company and your products. Management must be sure, if purchasing an outside list, that its customer characteristics are similar to those of present customers. Equally important is the development of an outstanding data base which details all information gathered during subsequent conversations and activities. To increase the odds of success, call present customers on a regular basis to take orders, offer additional services, or to determine customer satisfaction.

2. Sales call content: As in any endeavor, the final results will be directly related to the amount of effort put into the project. The script used in the sales pitch must be finely-honed, having undergone numerous revisions by the sales department. It is important that all necessary points are covered in a clear and concise manner. Anticipate possible questions and answer them.

3. Training of sales personnel: In the outbound telephone situation, where the primary purpose is to sell your product or

service, the communicator should be cautioned to stick to the prepared script. You must discourage any ad-libbing. If this is difficult to do, then your script is not fully developed. The caller should be polite, professional and call prospects who have a relevant need for your product. Do not waste anyone's time with a long, drawn-out pitch to someone who has no interest in, or time for, your company.

4. Evaluation: The telephone will provide immediate results. Scripts can be revised, or products added if the effort is proceeding successfully. Costs can be projected, and decisions can be made on an ongoing basis. Some of the by-products to be derived from telemarketing are:

- New information about the use of your product or sug-gestions for product improvements
- New trends valuable to long-range planning
- New leads in a given territory to assist salesmen in planning their itinerary

THE 800 NUMBER

The use of an 800 number can give the sales effort a shot in the arm. By inserting the 800 number in company correspondence you can increase the amount of customer activity dramatically. It also adds prestige and credibility to a company's image, can revive a poor-pulling ad, and can be used to direct customers to the nearest dealer. Some firms use the 800 number to screen and qualify incoming sales leads before quickly passing them on to salespeople for follow-up. It is also being used by many firms for customer-service for the purpose of building brand loyalty. Studies have shown that only a small percentage of dissatisfied customers will call to complain to a manufacturer. They will usually just stop buying the product.

Where complaints are received and resolved quickly, there will be a higher percentage of repeat purchases. Routine warranty problems can be handled on the telephone and in the process reduce costs by 33 to 50 percent as opposed to responding by letter. In the future those companies who do not offer this service might very well be at a significant disadvantage. By the same token, a poorly-planned and operated 800 line will quickly backfire! Callers become irritated with long waiting periods on "hold" no matter how pleasant the music is, and busy signals or operators who cannot answer routine questions will promptly lose customers. Consequently, it makes sense to test carefully and gradually implement this program.

INDUSTRIAL TELEMARKETING

If your company sells a product or service to the industrial marketplace, a solid telemarketing program can be a tremendous asset. Because industrial accounts usually represent a larger potential volume of business, there is a lot more at stake each time a contact is made. Telephone communicators will need thorough product knowledge, more briefings on market conditions and generally must be well-versed in order to be able to answer objections in a thorough and professional manner.

Industrial selling, compared to consumer sales, usually requires many more visits before a sale is made. As costs continue to increase, it simply makes good sense to take steps which will make every face-to-face call produce revenue. This is where the telemarketing group will pave the way for face-to-face sales call. They will do the following:

- Canvass, qualify and service the accounts to free up the salesforce so that they can do more face-to-face selling
- Perform the sales function in accounts which are geographically uneconomical to call on, or small and/or marginal

- Provide faster coverage when providing newsworthy developments to customers such as product improvements, or special sales programs

Because of the stakes involved in the telemarketing group, there is a greater importance in the development of the script and the control which will enable you to utilize successfully the information gathered. Scripts should be kept flexible. A word-for-word approach, as used in consumer selling is not practical. The script should be a guide because the industrial call is more complex. Word-for-word scripts should be used only for key parts of the pitch. Then the communicator can use his own style to present the rest of the story. The communicator should be provided with technical briefings on the produts he is selling. This will make him sound knowledgeable and cut down on the probability of his sounding like a recording. The script should contain responses that will answer customer objections. Chances are that the same general kinds of questions will continue to be asked, and after a period of familiarization, answers to these questions will become second nature.

Once the message has been developed, the all important control forms must be developed and utilized. The type of forms required include the following:

ACCOUNT CARDS - Providing general background data of the account

CALL LOGS - Briefly showing each call to each account and
the results

LITERATURE REQUEST FORMS

SALES CONFIRMATION AND FOLLOW-UP LETTERS

CALL-BACK SCHEDULING -- TO FOLLOW UP CALLS

The telephone communicators must essentially present the message, anticipate the questions, successfully answer them, and either close the sales or quickly pass it on to the salesforce for follow-up. The information the communicators must extract to be able to correctly evaluate a prospect is:

- Who makes the buying decisions?
- What factors affect those decisions?
- What brand does the customer currently buy?
- What price is he now paying?
- Is he satisfied?

It is a good idea to have supervisors constantly monitor the telephone conversations, whether they are live or taped, to assist the communicator in improving his performance and to make any necessary mofifications in strategy or scripts to enhance results.

Once a telemarketing program has been fully developed, do not get excited and go on a national scale right away! The program should be tested on a small regional scale to work the bugs out of the script, control forms, and customer lists. After you are satisfied with the regional results, move to a larger regional area and continue to make modifications as required. At this stage you should have enough information to make a fairly good projection of what a national program will cost and what it can produce, and you can decide whether to go national, stay the same, or discontinue the program.

Telemarketing has also been used by some firms to increase trade show selling. About 30 days prior to the show, calls are made to the better accounts urging them to attend. Once the trade show begins, the salesforce qualifies the prospect according to his requirements, interest, and ability to buy. Hot leads are contacted directly. Other leads are either put on a mailing list to receive mailings, or called by the telemarketing group to develop the prospects as future customers.

SUMMARY

The importance of an effective telemarketing program will continue to increase as selling costs escalate. It can be utilized to reduce the amount of face-to-face selling time by the field sales representative, by more closely qualifying and determining immediate customer needs. It can also allow for more frequent communications at a fraction of the cost, while building on customer relations.

Unless your operation is one where there is a constant flow of telephone activity, it does not pay to maintain an in-house staff. In such cases, outside firms providing this type of service can be hired on an as-needed basis. If your requirements call for an in-house telemarketing group, it would be wise to hire an outside experienced consultant to assist in forming the department. Important decisions must be made in such areas as equipment to be used, personnel, prospect lists, program development, and coordinating the effort with the end-user. A clearly defined objective must be identified at the very outset of the program. After the program has been instituted in selected local or regional areas, it should be reevaluated to determine the feasibility of expanding such a program to a national basis, or of maintaining it on a regional basis.

IX. DIRECT MAIL

Whenever someone asks what I would consider to be the most effective sequence of events to sell new customers, I always suggest direct mail, followed by telemarketing, and capped by a personal call. Direct mail is probably the most cost effective tool available to establish contact with prospective customers. Once a prospect responds to your mailings, he should be turned over to the telemarketing group for qualifications as to the degree of buying interest. It must then be determined if a salesman should follow up, if there is a chance of a sale. If it is likely that the prospect will purchase at some future point in time, he can be kept on the mailing list to receive future company mailings that will maintain his interest level.

If your business is in the retail field or performs a service, mailings can attract enough attention to get prospects to visit you at your location. For those customers who do not buy right away but indicate a willingness to do so in the future, public relations messages can enhance your company's prestige in the eyes of prospects, as well as employees or other selected groups. In instances where it may not be feasible to have a salesman call on a customer either because of geography and/or small order quantities, ordering merchandise can be handled exclusively via the mails. Another excellent use of direct mail is the conducting of research and market surveys of your customers to find out what they like about your products/services and how you can better service them. This is a great source of feedback available to all companies, yet few ever take time to utilize it.

I hope I have conveyed to you the tremendous advantage of using direct mail in your sales program. Once you have decided to use it, here are some of the basic guidelines to consider when planning and evaluating the program:

A. What do you want to accomplish?

Do you want to generate leads which will be further qualified by a telemarketing group? Do you want the direct mail piece to generate better qualified leads which will go directly to the salesman for follow-up; or are you asking the direct mail package to sell for you and bring back orders? In some markets you may want direct orders; while in others you may want only a good qualified lead. That is the beauty of direct mail. You can divide your campaign in any number or ways; according to different markets, geography, customer size, etc.

B.   What kind of mailing list(s) will you need?

Even after you have gone through the process of preparing your strategy and the materials to be used the entire effort can go down the drain by not mailing to the right list of prospects.   What is the ideal list for you to use?   Let's assume your company wants to sell a special type of gloves intended for those who handle hazardous materials at $75.00 per pair in a cash-with-order sale.   By working with a list broker, you would be able to come up with a list which would have the exact characteristics and conditions you are looking for in potential customers.   This is the kind of list you would want to rent.   It is far better to mail weak materials to the right list than to mail an excellent piece of literature to the wrong list.

Here are some points to remember:

1.   Zero in on Standard Industrial Classifications (SIC)
     Where is the first place to start? Your own customers! Start coding them to see where they fall.   One of the first determinants will be dictated by the SIC number where the greater portion of your customers fall.

2. Compiled list

If you are going to use these lists, the SIC numbers become even more important. Names on such lists, come from such sources such as phone books, newspapers, directories, trade show registrants, etc. Depending on what you expect from your mailings, these may or may not be the best kinds of lists to rent. These "prospects" may not have a need for your products, or they may not even believe in buying through the mails.

3. Personalized letters

Do not overlook the use of personalized letters to top executives, addressed by name and title, if you sell to the industrial markets. There have been numerous success stories using this approach. When choosing lists to be used in this mode, I must caution you to use extra care, because using a list with incorrect spellings or titles (Mr. when it should be Mrs.) can quickly diminish the very effect you are looking to create.

4. Merge-purge

This is the process of identifying and eliminating duplicated names on multiple lists you plan on using, or duplicated names of your current customers on a rented list. Not only will duplication inflate your cost of doing business, but prospects will be annoyed at receiving the same piece of mail three times! I have received one such mailing as many as four times. Imagine the cost of duplication in that campaign!

5. Benefits

The general tone of the mailings should stress the benefits you are offering the reader. Do not be shy! State facts not fiction! Offer statements with proofs and endorsements. Finally, tell the customer what he will lose if he does not take you up on your offer. Be sure to make it easy for the prospect to respond. Include your toll-free number, an order form with envelope, the selling price, and any other pertinent information needed.

6. Level of address

Always keep in mind to whom you are sending this mailing. The level of address (i.e., colloquial or formal) would be different if your mailings were to high school dropouts or to civil engineers. The layouts and graphics would also be affected by what you are trying to sell, a high-priced item or a low-priced item. Are you announcing a sale or trying to raise funds for a special cause?

7. Testing

Always look to improve the direct mail package! Test your
offers, products, copy approach, market segments, and the
timing of the mailings; but don't get hung up in testing such
trivial things as color of stationery, print style and so
forth.

USE OF DIRECT MAIL IN INDUSTRIAL MARKETS

The cost of sales calls continues to escalate annually.
Calling on industrial customers usually requires more sales calls
before a sale is realized. It is not unheard of to wait for periods
in excess of a year before a customer determines where and if he
will buy. Clearly this type of environment is ideal for a direct
mail program.

Let's examine the use of direct mail in the industrial
marketplace.

A. Public relations. Direct mail can be used to project positive
images of your company. It can keep readers informed about
new developments which can affect them, attract good personnel, and promote any point of view beneficial to your
business.

B. Product sales. Direct mail is most often used to sell a product. Among the many uses, here are the most frequent:

- to obtain leads from customers, and distributors
- to assist salesmen in reaching decision-making executives who are normally inaccessible
- to achieve brand recognition
- to present your whole sales story complete with applications and tie-ins
- to promote services
- to enter into and develop new markets (an ideal method)

C. Customer information up dates. Whether you use your own salesforce or outside agents, direct mail can be used to keep customers up to date on new sales approaches, markets, new applications, and promotions, etc.

D. Quick contacts. When an opportunity arises which requires quick action, direct mail lets you make all the necessary "contacts" in a short period of time.

The use of direct mail in the industrial marketplace can bridge the long expensive gap of the selling process. Maintaining an ongoing communication through newsletters and releases can cut down on the number of unnecessary field visits while sustaining the customer's interest until he is ready to act.

SELLING SERVICES BY DIRECT MAIL

If your business is one where you perform a service, there are numerous ways you can promote your services by using direct mail. Mailing a well-prepared letter with a specific reason for the mailing can enhance your opportunity of gaining new customers.

Here are some special opportunities for mailings:

- welcoming someone to a new city
- moving to a new address
- congratulating for a special achievement
- newlyweds and new children congratulations
- get-well wishes
- thanking for inquiring about your services
- holidays
- sympathy

WRITING DIRECT MAIL COPY

It is not the intention of this book to teach you how to write direct mail copy. My suggestion is to seek an experienced copywriter to put together a direct mail package which will enhance your direct mail program. I suggest you contact the Direct Mail Marketing Association (DMMA) in New York City and ask them to provide you with names of recommended copywriters.

If you must write your own copy, I strongly suggest that you go to the best library available in your area and research thoroughly the subject of copywriting. There are numerous good books on this subject. You may also write to the DMMA and ask them for their suggestions as well.

SALES BROCHURES

Sales brochures are sometimes referred to as "the quiet salesman". Long after the salesman has made his presentation and answered all the questions, the sales brochure remains. Undoubtedly, the prospect will glance at it again after the salesman has left, to re-enforce his belief or disbelief in your product. Consequently, the brochure must continue to sell.

When putting together a sales brochure, remember the following points:

- If your product is of a technical nature, make sure all technical data is given, to provide decision-makers with all relevant information needed to properly evaluate your product.
- Design the brochure so that the salesman can use it in his presentation. This will assure the salesman that he has covered all the important points. The brochure also serves as a reminder of key features when the prospect reviews it at a later date.
- Briefly state the benefits of your product or service. Do not overwhelm the prospect with mountains of unimportant data. The benefits should be summarized again towards the end of the brochure.
- Show pictures of your product. If your product is of a technical nature show detailed pictures. Show pictures of your product solving problems. Make sure they are quality pictures. Make them look "glamorous".
- Make the brochure easy to follow. Violate this principle and you will have a bunch of useless paper.

- If the brochure is also to be used for your direct mail program, it should include a promotional letter, perhaps with a teaser message on the envelope.

Whether your sales program does or does not utilize a direct mail program, a good sales brochure is a selling tool which cannot be overlooked.

CATALOGS

Another popular and growing area of direct mail is selling through catalogs. Using this tool to present your full range of products while providing all essential product features has quickly become a major profit source in many firms. Do not neglect to include your most popular selling products. After all, you are trying to generate the most revenue for your investment while adding new customers.

If you are trying to sell to different market segments, do not try to do it all with the same catalog. Design a different catalog for each market segment emphasizing not only different sets of product features, but perhaps additional products as well. An effective catalog builds benefits into every headline. The emphasis should be in areas where there is interest and a perception of value. When describing benefits don't indulge in pointless puffery, name specific user benefits. Catalog selling programs are an excellent alternative to combat the escalating cost of personal sales calls.

SUMMARY

The use of direct marketing continues to increase in the business community because of its ability to increase selling effectiveness while proportionately reducing costs. The ability to segment customer groups will allow your selling message to reach only those prospects who have a genuine interest in, or need for, what you have to sell. By combining direct marketing with a solid telemarketing program, the level of effectiveness will be elevated to even greater heights.

Probably the area of greatest need for direct marketing is in the industrial marketplace, where a customer can take months, if not longer, before he makes a buying decision. Great care must be taken in selecting a customer list before making your mailings. Ideally when choosing a customer list, try to choose lists which have the same characteristics as your own customer base to ensure good reception of your sales message.

CONCLUSION

As the cost of doing business continues to increase, it is up to decision-makers to review their own operation and determine what can be done to increase the return on their investment. A periodic thorough review of all sales activities, comparing costs and results, will provide the benchmarks necessary to accurately evaluate the level of effectiveness.

A cold hard look must be taken at the traditional sales approaches, such as relying on cold canvassing as the greater portion of a prospecting program for new customers. Is the salesman spending his time wisely, or is he wasting a large portion of his time by knocking on door after door in the hope of finding a "hot" lead? Selling is a highly emotional act, and cold canvassing is a very humbling activity, which can wear down the positive attitude necessary to succeed in the selling game.

Can your firm benefit from some modifications in its selling programs? Probably. The starting point should be in personnel. Decide what can be done to upgrade the caliber of sales personnel entering the company. No worthwhile program is easy to institute, however, keeping any organization fat-free will become even more important in the future as costs continue to escalate and competition stiffens. Do you have any doubts that this will occur? I simply ask that you go back and look at your own company and industry ten to fifteen years ago and see the changes which have taken place.

Today, we are asking everything to work harder for us, from the advertising dollar to finding more effective fulfillment systems. Consequently, more effective methods of finding, qualifying and selling new customers must be at the forefront of any selling program. We must put the salesman in more face-to-face pure selling situations to increase his chances of generating more revenues, which should in a general sense increase the dollar return on investments. How can we accomplish this? By having an effective direct mail program which generates good quality leads. These leads are further qualified by a telemarketing group to determine their value either on a short or long-term basis. By providing the salesforce with these leads, you supplement their own prospecting activities and foster an atmosphere where increased productivity is the synthesis of their efforts and your own.

Increasing the level of communication can lend itself to increasing cooperation between the different departments within a company. To be totally effective, the support staff must have a clear understanding of what is occurring out in the field. This necessitates their visiting customers along with the salesmen and/or attending sales meetings. The salesmen should not be in a position where they have to fight with their own personnel to gain their cooperation to perform their jobs. Here is where management must lay the groundwork to create an environment where a free flow of information moves in both directions to keep all those involved fully aware of all activities. The scenario described is one which is needed not only to enhance the selling effort, but one which is increasingly important if your company is to remain competitive in the marketplace in years to come.

Success comes to those who are constantly re-evaluating for methods and/or angles which they can apply to their own situation. With this in mind, I am publishing a bi-monthly sales journal, with each issue examining in depth a different facet of the sales and marketing process. Such areas as: sales promotion, advertising, customer behavior, the legal aspects of selling, pricing concepts and practices, customer segmentation, distribution of goods, and international selling will be included. I trust you will find them informative and useful to you in assisting you in running your business more effectively. The publication, entitled <u>The Feris-Lee Sales Journal</u>, is available through the publisher of this book, Feris-Lee, Press, Lodi, New Jersey.

APPENDIX A

TELEMARKETING ASSISTANCE

The following is a sample of the firms which provide telemarketing assistance in managing sales leads.

American Response and Management

PO Box 430, Battle Creek, MI 49016   (616) 96 -2221

Provides complete marketing support systems, including computerized management of leads.

Visions, Inc.

PO Box 5214, Lancaster, PA 17601   (717) 291-1825

Offers complete lead qualification service.

Inquiry Handling Service, Inc.

15540 Roxfort St., Sylman, CA 91342   (213) 362-5873

Provides complete detailed reports on prospects and follow-up service, if desired.

Inquiry Systems and Analysis

35 Morrissey Blvd., Boston, MA 02125   (617) 265-8338

Offer sales-lead processing, and management reporting.   Also can provide fulfillment, sales tracking, and program development.

Telemarketing Assistance Program/AT&T

Contact AT&T Telemarketing Sales Center: (201) 939-4500

Provides analysis and training in lead qualification. Can also provide product information, order processing and customer service for companies thinking about a telemarketing program.

Leadtrack Corp.

1709 Mount Vernon Rd., Suite 4, Atlanta, GA 30333

(404)393-3690

Offers a software package designed to fulfill and track sales leads. Also makes arrangements for those without computer facilities.

Leads-Plus/Mr. Mailer, Inc.

2471 John Young Pkwy., Orlando, FL 32804 (305) 295-6767

Provides detailed instruction on how to prospect through direct mail and telephone techniques.

QLS/The Qualified Lead System

23 East 22nd St., New York, NY 10010 (212) 505-7900

Provides telephone qualifications of leads gathered from advertising, trade shows, publicity, etc.

Creative Computer Services, Inc.

10804 N. Stemmons Freeway, Dallas, TX 75220   (214) 358-4493

Provides fulfillment of inquiries, tracking for salespeople,

contact follow-up, and detailed analysis of all needs.

Tele America, Inc.

1955 Raymond Dr., Suite 112, Northbrook, ILL 60062

(312) 480-1560

Provides assistance in inquiry handling and qualification,

follow-up, direct mail, marketing research, and toll-free

response programs.

Telesales Technology, Inc.

PO Box 10967, Suite 500, Houston, TX 77292   (713) 688-4812

Service includes lead generation, follow-up, tracking,

development, and all facets of record keeping with customized

programs.

Wats Marketing Outbound

Wats Marketing of America

3105-3250 N. 93rd St., Omaha, NE 68134

Outbound; 1 800 348-1000

America; 1 800 351-1000

Outbound - Offers a large variety of sales and research services. America - Offers a network of toll-free numbers that allows gathering of responses and in-house follow-up. Also offers inbound services as well.

Sales Management Systems
50 Church St., Cambridge, MA   (617) 492-1571
Provides leads and information in the salesforce by means of personal computers.

New York Telmarketing Group
61-47 188 St., Fresh Meadows, New York, NY 11365
(718) 479-3700
Provides assistance with direct mail, prospecting, qualifying of leads, market research and customer service. Also in-house service to companies who do not want to develop their own systems.

APPENDIX B

GOVERNMENT PUBLICATIONS

When planning sales strategy, it is imperative to check some of the census publications published by the Bureau of Census. Here are some of the most popular references used. The government publications listed can be purchased by writing to Superintendent of Documents, U.S. Government Printing Office, Washington, DC 20402

MEASURING MARKETS: A guide to the use of federal and state statistical data. Bureau of Domestic and International Business Administration, Department of Commerce. Revised periodically. This reference describes federal and state government publications useful for measuring markets but also demonstrates the use of federal statistics in market measurement.

STATISTICAL ABSTRACT OF THE UNITED STATES. BUREAU OF CENSUS, DEPARTMENT OF COMMERCE: This comprehensive and authoritative data book on social, economic, and government characteristics of the United States. Special features include selections on recent national trends and an appendix on statistical methodology and reliability.

COUNTY AND CITY DATA BOOK, BUREAU OF CENSUS, DEPARTMENT OF COM-
MERCE: A total of 195 Statistical items tabulated for the U.S.,
its regions, and each county and state; 190 items for each city;
and 161 items for 277 Standard Metropolitan Statistical Areas.
Information is derived from the latest available census of population, housing, governments, mineral industries, agriculture,
manufactures, retail and wholesale trade, and selected services.
It also includes data on health, vital statistics, public assistance programs, bank deposits, votes cast for president, and crime.

A GUIDE TO CONSUMER MARKETS: The Conference Board, Inc., 45 3rd
Ave., New York, NY 10022. Provides detailed statistical profile
of U.S. consumers markets. It contains data on population growth
and mobility, employment, income, consumer spending patterns,
production and sales prices.

SM&M SURVEY OF BUYING POWER: Revised annually by Sales and
Marketing Management, 633 3rd Ave., New York, NY 10017. Information includes current estimates of population and households by
income groups, total effective buying income, retail sales for
major retail lines, and market quality indexes; given for all
regions, states, counties, and metropolitan areas.

COUNTY BUSINESS PATTERNS. DEPARTMENT OF COMMERCE. Separate book for each state, District of Columbia, and a U.S. summary. It reports figures on first quarter employment, first quarter payroll, annual payroll, number of establishments by employment size class for some 700 different U.S. business and industries by each county in the U.S.

SALES AND MARKETING MANAGEMENT'S SURVEY OF SELLING COST: Revised annually in February. Sales and Marketing Management, 633 3rd Ave., New York, NY 10017. Contains data on cost of sales meetings and sales training, metro sales cost for major U.S. markets, compensation, sales-support activities and transportation.

Maps play an important function in the overall sales effort. here are some excellent sources of supply:

AMERICAN MAP CO., 1926 Broadway, New York, NY 10023. Send away for their catalog of clear type and colorprint maps.

RAND McNALLY & CO., PO Box 7600, Chicago, ILL 60623. Publishes a variety of maps and atlases. It leases a commercial atlas and marketing guide, which contains maps showing counties and cities, a road atlas, and statistical data on manufacturing, retail sales, and population. Standard Metropolitan areas shown, including a city index.

SALES BUILDERS, 633 3rd Ave., New York, NY 10017. It publishes two sets of regional maps which have county outlines and depict either the consumer or manufacturing data.

FERIS-LEE, PRESS, PO Box 560, Lodi, NJ 07644-0560. Publishes bi-monthly sales journal ($59.00 per year) providing valuable insight into the many aspects of a successful sales and marketing program.

APPENDIX C

SOURCES OF NEW PRODUCTS

I.   Government owned patents; Government owned patents are available on a non-exclusive, royalty-free basis. Some government agencies will issue a license with some degree of exclusivity if no license has been requested after 2 years from the date of patent. Information on government owned patents may be obtained from your local Small Business Administration office nearest you, or write to the U.S. Patent Office, Department of Commerce, Washington, DC 20231.

II. Patent Abstract Bibliography (PAB). This is a semi-annual publication listing NSA-owned patents and applications for patents as a service for those seeking new licensable products for the commercial market. PAB may be ordered from the National Technical Information Service (NTIS), U.S. Department of Commerce, Springfield, VA 22151.

III. ABC-NASA Tech Briefs are 1 or 2 page descriptions of ideas, concepts, or patents for new products, innovations, applications, or process. They are the result of work performed by, or under contract to, the Atomic Energy Commission or the National Aeronautics and Space Administration. Your local SBA office can provide you with additional information on them.

IV. Government Report Announcements and Index are current awareness announcements published semi-monthly. The announcements may be ordered from NTIS.

V. Private Patents - The official Gazette of the U.S. Patent Office is published weekly and lists all the patents granted by the Patents office. Contact the Superintendent of Documents, Government Printing Office, Washington, DC 20402.

There are also a number of private publications available for sale or licensing, which list patents. Check your local library. Patent attorneys are another source of new products.

VI. Large Corporations - Most large corporations, especially aerospace firms develop many new products. However, many of these products although highly desirable may not be suitable for their own operations for many reasons. Sometimes these large firms maintain a separate department for the sole purpose of finding suitable licensees. They may also be able to provide market studies, manufacturing know-how, and other pertinent information or services to reduce the risk to the company seeking the products.

VII. Inventory Shows - The Chambers of Commerce in large metropolitan areas generally sponsor these types of shows to allow manufacturers and inventors to get together to put new products on the market. Check with your local Chamber of Commerce office or write to the Office of the Inventions and Innovations, National Bureau of Standards, Washington, DC 20234.

VIII. Commercial Banks - By talking with your commercial banker, you may be able to learn about a company which may need the strengths of your company to become successful.

IX. Small Business Investment Company (SBIC) and Investment Bankers - Contact with these kinds of firms can lead to a new product or an equity position in a business with a solid product. Your local SBA office can furnish you with a list of licensed SBIC's in your area.

X. Licensing Brokers - They will usually represent companies seeking licensees as well as those searching for a product to license. They may also have a wide experience in developing fair and reasonable licensing agreements and can advise their clients accordingly.

XI. Foreign Licenses - The U.S. Department of Commerce publishes weekly "The International Commerce Magazine". It contains a licensing opportunies section which lists foreign products seeking U.S. firms to manufacture and sell products to the U.S. market. This may be ordered through the Department of Commerce local field office.

XII. New Product Advertising - Trade or industry periodicals and financial newspapers often carry ads of new products available to a manufacturer. You can also place an advertisement seeking new products.

ABOUT THE AUTHOR

Mr. Sanchez has a B.S. degree from New Hampshire College and holds an M.B.A. from St. John's University. He has held sales and sales management positions with several Fortune 500 firms, and has served as a consultant to management.

FOOTNOTES

1. Training Salesmen to Serve Industrial Markets, U.S. Small Business Administration Publication Number 36.

2. Training Salesmen to Serve Industrial Markets.

3. Preventing Drug Abuse in the Work Place, Published by U.S. Department of Health and Human Services, Public Health Service, Alcohol, Drug Abuse, and Mental Health Administration.

4. Marketing for Small Business, Small Business Bibliography Number 89. Published by U.S. Small Business Administration.

5. Delegating Work and Responsibility, Management Aids Number 3.001. Published by U.S. Small Business Administration.

6. Techniques for Productivity Improvement, Management Aid 5.009. Published by U.S. Small Business Administration.

7. Techniques for Problem Solving, Management Aid Number 3.010. Published by U.S. Small Business Administration.

8. Developing New Accounts, Management Aid Number 4.010. Published by U.S. Small Business Administration.

9. Creative Selling: The Competitive Edge, Management Aid Number 4.002. Published by U.S. Small Business Administration.

10. Measuring Sales Performance, Management Aid 4.003. Published by U.S. Small Business Administration.

11. Is the Independent Sales Agent for You? Management Aid Number 4.005. Published by U.S. Small Business Administration.

12. Selling Products on Consignement. Management Aid Number 4.007. Published by U.S. Small Business Administration.